Understanding September 11th

ANSWERING QUESTIONS

ABOUT THE ATTACKS ON AMERICA

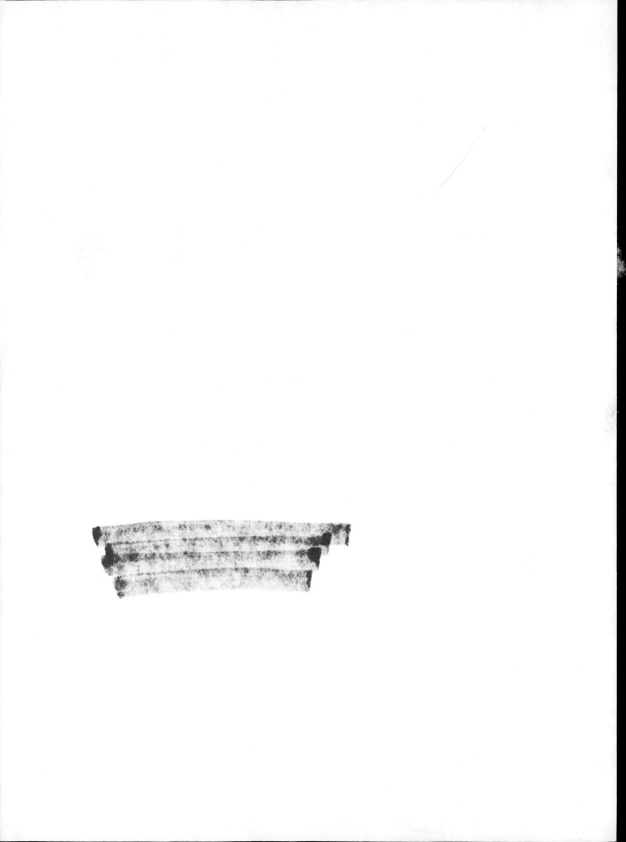

Understanding September 11th

ANSWERING QUESTIONS

ABOUT THE ATTACKS ON AMERICA

by Mitch Frank

VIKING

VIKING

Published by Penguin Group

Penguin Young Readers Group, 345 Hudson Street, New York, New York 10014, U.S.A.

Penguin Books Ltd, 80 Strand, London WC2R ORL, England

Penguin Books Australia Ltd, Ringwood, Victoria, Australia

Penguin Books Canada Ltd, 10 Alcorn Avenue, Toronto, Ontario, Canada M4V 3B2

Penguin Books (N.Z.) Ltd, 182-190 Wairau Road, Auckland 10, New Zealand

First published in 2002 by Viking, a division of Penguin Putnam Books for Young Readers.

10 9 8 7 6 5 4 3

Copyright © Mitch Frank, 2002

LIBRARY OF CONGRESS CATALOGING-IN-PUBLICATION DATA

Frank, Mitch.

Understanding September 11th : answering questions about the attacks on America / by Mitch Frank.

p.   cm.

Summary: Explains the historical and religious issues that sparked terrorists to attack America on September 11, 2001, including information on Islam, Osama bin Laden, and the Middle East.

ISBN 0-670-03582-3 (hardcover)—ISBN 0-670-03587-4 (pbk.)

1. September 11 Terrorist Attacks, 2001—Juvenile literature. 2. Terrorism—United States—Juvenile literature. 3. Bin Laden, Osama, 1957—Juvenile literature. 4. World politics—1995-2005—Juvenile literature. [1. September 11 Terrorist Attacks, 2001. 2. Terrorism. 3. Bin Laden, Osama, 1957- 4. World politics—1995-2005.] I. Title: Understanding September eleventh. II. Title.

HV6432 .F735 2002   973.931—dc21   2002001725

Printed in the U.S.A. / Set in Century Expanded

Book design by Nancy Brennan

Photo Credits

© AFP/CORBIS, pp. 22, 43, 83, 89, 94, 115, 122. © Bettmann/CORBIS, pp. 30, 39, 69. © Mitch Frank, p. xii. © Owen Franken/CORBIS, p. 57. © Philip Greenberg, p. 7. © Earl & Nazima Kowall/CORBIS, p. 102. © Charles & Josette Lenars/CORBIS, p. 74. © Matt McDermott/CORBIS SYGMA, p. 119. © Caroline Penn/CORBIS, p. 62. © Reuters NewMedia Inc./CORBIS, pp. 19, 100, 109. © David Rubinger/CORBIS, p. 28. © Bill Vaughn/CORBIS SYGMA, p. 11. © David H. Wells/CORBIS, p. 53.

Map Credits

© Rick Britton, pp. 46, 54-55, 75.

THIS BOOK IS DEDICATED to the people of New York City. Your strength has shown everyone that this is the greatest city in the world.

And also to the brave people at the Pentagon, who ignored their own wounds to lead the nation into battle; and to the people of Afghanistan, who know far too well what war and pain mean.

Contents

Introduction 1

1. What happened on September 11th? 5

2. Who were the hijackers? 17

3. What is terrorism? 24

4. What is Islam? 36

   Map: The Early Spread of Islam 46

5. Why does the Middle East matter to us? 51

   Map: The Middle East and Central Asia 54-55

6. Why did the terrorists target the United States? 60

7. Why did we go after Afghanistan? 72

   Map: Afghanistan and Surrounding Region 75

8. Who are the Taliban? 84

9. What is Islamism? 98

10. Who is Osama bin Laden? 108

11. How has America changed since September 11th? 117

   Glossary 126

   Bibliography 131

   Index 133

The author photographed the burning twin towers of the World Trade Center near City Hall in downtown Manhattan on September 11th, 2001.

Introduction

I CAN STILL remember the boom of the first explosion. I wish I had known at the time what it meant. But when you live in New York City, it's not that odd to hear the occasional boom outside your apartment window. I just figured it was construction, a little loud but not out of the ordinary. But it was the sound of a commercial airliner slamming into the north tower of the World Trade Center. It was the sound that announced that nothing would be the same in my city again. It was the sound that woke America up. It was a little before nine A.M. on September 11th, 2001.

I live in Brooklyn Heights, right across the East River from downtown Manhattan, where the World Trade Center stood. It's a beautiful neighborhood, long prized for the views of downtown with its incredible skyscrapers. The twin towers loomed above all of those buildings like parents to skyscraper children. They were enormous. When I used to walk through the streets near my apartment, I would come out from behind a building and suddenly those towers would loom into view, and they were always much bigger than I anticipated.

But the first time I saw them that morning was on TV. Ten minutes after that loud boom, the north tower was on my television screen. The news anchors were trying to figure out what had happened. My mind went back to a picture I had seen of a bomber plane that crashed into the top of the Empire State Building during World War II. It had lost its way in the fog. Maybe some small plane or helicopter had accidentally plowed into the tower? I sat in amazement for five minutes before I remembered I was a reporter for *Time* magazine. It was my job to go out there and find out what happened. The thought upset me—it was a horrible scene. But dreading it wouldn't make it go away. I grabbed my camera and my bag and ran for the door.

Two blocks from my apartment, I heard the second boom.

I ran to where I could see the towers and saw a fireball rising up from the south tower. Witnesses described to me how a second plane had flown straight into it. Suddenly this was no horrible accident. This was an attack. I sprinted to the Brooklyn Bridge, which leads across to Manhattan. The whole time, my mind was trying to catch up to what had happened. After interviewing more witnesses, I began to quickly walk across the bridge, through streams of people fleeing Manhattan like refugees. I thought every sound was another plane. I started to understand what it must feel like to cover a war.

On the other side of the bridge was utter chaos. A third of the people were heading for Brooklyn the way I had come, a third were walking uptown, and a third were standing in the street and staring in awe at the towers. Two fiery holes burned in the sides of the mighty buildings, and a long cloud of the blackest smoke I had ever seen drifted slowly across the East River toward Brooklyn. Papers were fluttering toward the earth. I am thankful that I never saw the many people who jumped out of the windows to get away from the flames. Two police officers stood next to their squad car, asking people to move uptown. I asked one if an evacuation plan had been put in place. He pointed across the street to City Hall and told me to go ask there. I spoke to a couple crouched around a radio, who told me the Pentagon had been hit. Everyone was in a daze of shock and confusion.

I kept walking closer to the towers, stopping three blocks away from them, where a barricade of police were blocking the way. For fifteen minutes, we all just stood there and stared. A woman ran up to the police, frantically telling them her brother worked in the south tower and she had to find him. A few of us took her aside, trying to calm her down, telling her we were sure he was fine. She couldn't stop crying. It seemed like things couldn't get worse.

And then we all heard a loud groan. The crowd screamed. At first the top of the south tower teetered—it looked as if it might fall on us. We all just stood frozen, helpless. But instead it plunged straight down in a horrific implosion. The tower was gone in less than thirty seconds. But those seconds have been with me ever since, because as it went down I realized that more than a thousand people were probably still inside. It disappeared into a cloud of dust and noise and smoke. And that cloud began to roll toward us like a tidal wave. It was only then that we all turned and ran.

I made it fifty feet before the cloud swallowed me. Day became night. My mouth and nose filled with ash and dust. I just stopped and hoped it would pass. Thirty seconds later it did. We all started running again. Up Broadway we ran, cops yelling to head north, as they sprinted with us. A plane flew overhead. I found out later it was a fighter jet, coming to defend us from any more attacks. But as it roared overhead, people screamed that there was another suicide plane, and the crowd threatened to stampede. Finally we reached a safe distance. Some kept going. The rest of us turned around. Most of New York—and much of the country— was looking at the cloud where there had once been two towers. Now there was just one, half hidden by the dust. Forty minutes later it would be gone, too.

Two hours, that's all it took. Two hours, and New York changed forever. I spent the rest of the day covering the aftermath, numb with the thought of what I had seen. But thankfully I was too busy to think much. I spoke to rescue workers desperate to be able to get downtown and find their comrades. I spoke to doctors waiting outside hospitals for patients who never came. The rest of the city was in a daze. How had this happened? Why? Strangers began to help one another, offering water to drink, phones to use to get in touch with loved ones. People began to find their way home. But the questions were just beginning.

This book tries to answer some of those questions. Who were these men who were willing to sacrifice their own lives to kill thousands of innocent people on a sunny September day? Where did they come from? What did they want?

America is the most powerful nation on earth. But it is a nation that has sometimes resisted getting involved in world affairs. We have often felt the world was a complicated place and thought it was more important to worry about problems here at home. But events in far-off places can have dramatic consequences for us here. America may be an ocean away from most of the world, but we all share the same planet. Many people said the whole world changed on September 11th. It didn't. America woke up in those two hours and suddenly saw the world in a different light.

There has been some resistance to understanding why these terrorists attacked America. Some have felt that by trying to understand their motives, we are excusing what they did. Nothing could be further from the truth. There is nothing good in the hatred that led to these attacks. But you can change only what you understand. By understanding how this happened, we can defeat the terrorists and work to ensure history does not repeat itself.

1.
What happened on September 11th?

ON SEPTEMBER 11th, 2001, America was attacked. Terrorists hijacked four airplanes and flew one into each of the twin towers of the World Trade Center in New York City and one into the side of the Pentagon near Washington D.C. The fourth crashed into a field in Pennsylvania. More than three thousand people died.

On September 11th, America changed in two hours. The attacks ended what had been a decade of relative peace in this country. Americans suddenly realized that our own country, which had always seemed safe, was vulnerable to groups that hate us for our beliefs, our foreign policy, or just because we are Americans. It also made us realize how small the world is, that what happens in countries far away can have deadly consequences here at home. It was an awakening, and America will never be the same.

On September 11th, Mohammed Atta got up early. He was on an airplane flying from Portland, Maine, to Boston by about 6 A.M. Atta was one of five Middle Eastern men who boarded an American Airlines jet in Boston bound for Los Angeles. Shortly after it took off at 8 A.M., the five men used small knives they had smuggled past security to take over the plane. They stabbed two flight attendants and a passenger. They opened the cockpit door and killed the two pilots. Atta and another terrorist had learned how to fly planes while living in the United States. So they took over the controls, turning the plane south and heading toward New York City. They told all the passengers to stay calm; they were heading back to the airport.

On September 11th, it was a sunny day in New York City. At 8:47 A.M. some people looked up and saw a large 767 flying very low over the city. Before they could wonder why, the plane flew straight into the ninety-second floor of the north tower of the Trade Center. There was an enormous explosion. When the smoke cleared, there was a giant hole ten stories high in the side of the building. A large fire began to burn in the top twenty floors. Black smoke billowed out of the hole, and jet fuel and plane parts came spilling out, falling to the plaza below. To the people who witnessed the crash, it looked like a horrible accident. Firefighters and ambulances hurried downtown toward the towers. People watched from the streets or from office windows. Television crews began filming the towers within five minutes of the crash.

But there were three other hijacked planes in the sky by then. The second was a United Airlines jet that had been going from Boston to Los Angeles before it was hijacked. Another five-man team, this one led by Marwan al Shehhi, a close friend of Atta's, used knives to take control of the plane. They flew south of New York City, then turned around. Fifteen minutes after the first jet hit the north tower, the second sliced into the south tower, crashing into the eightieth floor. Suddenly New Yorkers realized this was not an accident. And there were two other hijacked planes still in the sky. At 9:41 A.M., commuters stuck in traffic outside Washington D.C. looked up to see a 757 fly low over the highway and slam

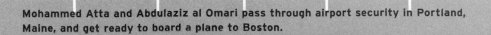

Mohammed Atta and Abdulaziz al Omari pass through airport security in Portland, Maine, and get ready to board a plane to Boston.

Desperate to escape Manhattan after the World Trade Center towers were hit, many New Yorkers left any way they could. These people crossed the Brooklyn Bridge on foot.

12:00   1:00   2:00   3:00   4:00   5:00   6:00

9/11/01
PM

Facts about the Twin Towers

THE BUILDINGS: Height: 110 floors each. The south tower (WTC 2) stood 1,368 feet tall; the north tower (WTC 1) was 6 feet shorter but had a 360-foot antenna on top for TV, radio, and cellular-phone signals. For two years, they were the tallest buildings on earth, until the Sears Tower in Chicago was built. **FLOOR SPACE:** An average of 45,000-50,000 square feet per floor **OCCUPANTS:** 50,000 people **ELEVATORS:** 103 in each tower, some local and some express **STEEL:** 200,000 tons (enough to build twenty Eiffel Towers) **CONCRETE:** 425,000 cubic yards (enough to build a sidewalk from the World Trade Center to the Pentagon) **WINDOWS:** 43,600 **TOILETS:** 7,000 **DOORKNOBS:** 40,000

into the side of the Pentagon. The fourth jet, another 757, had been seized by four hijackers and was heading toward Washington when it crashed into a field in Pennsylvania. Investigators suspect it was heading toward the U.S. Capitol building or the White House, though no one knows for sure. Several passengers on this plane had called their families on cell phones. After hearing what happened to the other planes, some of the passengers decided to attack the hijackers. During the struggle in the cockpit, the plane flipped and slammed into the ground. All on board died.

In New York, people were trying to get out of the twin towers as quickly as possible. Many called their loved ones from the emergency stairwells or from offices. Some were never heard from again. Firefighters were running up the stairs—some to help people evacuate the building, others to try and control the blaze on the upper floors. Many people were trapped on the floors above the flames, and when the heat became too intense, some jumped out the windows. Witnesses watching

5:00   6:00   7:00   ▼ 8:00 A.M.   9:00   10:00   11:00

American Airlines Flight 11 leaves Logan Airport in Boston bound for Los Angeles with 81 passengers and 11 crew members on board.

on the street could see them falling to their deaths. But the worst was yet to come. At 9:50 A.M., with an estimated thousand people still inside, the south tower collapsed. The jet fuel from the plane had created fires as hot as 2,000 degrees Fahrenheit. The steel and concrete on the burning floors melted. They couldn't support the weight of the floors above them. Those upper floors crashed down on top of the lower floors, and soon the entire building crumbled and came straight down. A huge cloud of dust and ash

A Brief History of the World Trade Center

■ The twin towers were just two of seven buildings in the World Trade Center, which also had an enormous underground complex complete with a shopping mall, two subway stations, and a station for commuter trains to New Jersey.

■ The towers were nicknamed David and Nelson for the two Rockefeller brothers who began the campaign in 1960 to build them in an effort to bring more business to downtown Manhattan. David was a wealthy businessman, Nelson the governor of New York.

■ The architect, Minoru Yamasaki, was an unlikely choice to build two skyscrapers. He was 5'1" and scared of heights. He came up with the idea of two towers as a symbol of working together. The towers were finished in 1972 and 1973. They were not very popular at first—people thought they were boxy and boring. But as people got used to them, these towering twins became a beloved sight. And they did begin a run of new construction downtown, revitalizing New York's financial district.

■ In 1993, terrorists supported by al Qaeda detonated a car bomb in the parking garage beneath the buildings. More than one hundred people were injured and six died. The explosion left a crater that could have weakened WTC 1, so construction crews worked for several weeks to make it safe again.

rose from the collapsing building and began to blanket the surrounding area. Those watching in the streets nearby ran as the cloud covered them and turned the sky dark. Once it cleared, police and firefighters began urging everyone to get out of the area. If one tower could collapse, the other could too. Only forty minutes later, it did.

Outside Washington, in northern Virginia, the west side of the Pentagon was burning as employees evacuated the entire building. One of the largest office buildings in the world, with 23,000 military and civilian staff members, the Defense Department's headquarters now had a five-story hole on one side, where army and navy personnel had offices. Hundreds were trapped inside. Those who escaped began to try to rescue their coworkers. A makeshift hospital was set up on the grass outside. As day turned to night, the fire was still burning. Eventually, the entire section collapsed. Inside the rubble, 125 people had died. That part of the building had recently been renovated, and workers had just begun to move back into their offices. A few weeks later, two thousand more lives might have been lost.

In New York, it would be hours before rescue workers could safely approach the massive pile of rubble where the towers once stood, to try to find survivors. Five other buildings near the towers were either partially or completely destroyed by the falling wreckage. One of those, the forty-seven-story 7 World Trade Center, collapsed at 5:20 P.M., after burning for most of the day. Doctors and nurses at hospitals throughout the city had started preparing for hundreds of patients immediately after the first plane hit. After treating some victims rescued before the buildings collapsed, they sat and waited. Very few patients arrived. Thousands of people were trapped underneath the rubble of the towers.

Meanwhile, the entire country was on alert and watching, wondering if

5:00   6:00   7:00   8:00   ▼ 8:14 A.M.   9:00   10:00   11:00

9/11/01
A M

United Airlines Flight 175 to Los Angeles leaves Boston with 56 passengers and 9 crew members on board.

The portion of the Pentagon that was directly hit eventually collapsed, after burning for several hours. Thousands of workers in the building were able to evacuate to safety before it fell.

there would be any more attacks. All nonmilitary planes were forced to land. The White House and Capitol building in Washington were evacuated. President George W. Bush had been meeting with elementary school students in Florida. Concerned he might be a target, the military got him aboard Air Force One quickly. On a secure military base in Louisiana, he came on television to ask Americans to remain calm. That evening, he returned to the White House and told the nation that this was a terrorist

12:00 1:00 2:00 3:00 4:00 5:00 6:00

attack, and that America would find whoever was responsible and punish them.

In New York, workers began digging through the rubble. Firefighters, knowing many of their comrades were buried underneath, dug hard. Volunteers from all over the city—police officers, construction workers, truck drivers, medics, and people who just wanted to help— began to look through the pieces of the World Trade Center. But fewer than a dozen survivors were found. After the first forty-eight hours, no one was found alive.

Who died in the attacks?

THERE WERE 266 passengers and crew members on board the four airplanes, including the 19 hijackers. No one on the planes lived. For the hijackers it was a suicide mission. The passengers included businessmen, a computer programmer, a gym coach, a television producer, two scouts from a hockey team, and a store manager. There were three sixth-grade students, accompanied by three teachers from a Washington D.C. school, who had won a contest and were on a trip to California. In the Pentagon, 125 Defense Department workers died, some military and some civilian.

Close to three thousand people died in the twin towers. The victims were as diverse as America. There were stockbrokers and janitors, lawyers and waiters and accountants, moms and dads, husbands and wives. And they were as multicultural as New York City. Visitors from eighty different countries died while working or sightseeing in the towers. Many police officers and paramedics were killed, and 343 firefighters died. Previously, only 778 New York City firefighters had died in the line of

5:00   6:00   7:00   8:00   9:00   10:00   11:00

▼ 8:21 A.M.

9/11/01
A.M.
American Airlines Flight 77 leaves Washington Dulles Airport bound for Los Angeles with 58 passengers and 6 crew members on board.

duty since the department was founded in 1865. The firefighters who died on the 11th had gone into the towers to save people. Many of the survivors remember seeing those firefighters running up the staircases as they were rushing down.

For the families and friends of the missing, the next few weeks were awful. First they visited hospitals, seeing if their loved ones had been taken there for treatment. If they didn't hear from them in the next few days, they went to a center the city set up where they provided their missing loved ones' name and lengthy descriptions so if they were found they could be identified. Some people brought hair with them so the authorities would have DNA samples of the missing. It might help if bodies were found that could not be otherwise identified. The DNA was meant to help identify bodies, but it would be months before many bodies were even found.

Was this the worst attack in U.S. history?

BY FAR. While America has faced wars and terrorist attacks overseas for most of our history, our home soil has been remarkably safe. The last major invasion of the United States was in 1812, when British troops landed in several locations and even burned the White House. But few civilians were killed. When Japanese planes attacked Pearl Harbor in 1941, drawing the U.S. into World War II, 2,400 sailors and soldiers died. But Pearl Harbor was in Hawaii, then a U.S. territory and far away from mainland America. And, unlike at Pearl Harbor, the majority of the more than three thousand people who died on September 11th were not soldiers but civilians.

The most deadly terrorist attack on America before September 11th was in 1995, when Timothy McVeigh, an American army veteran, detonated a bomb outside the Alfred P. Murrah Federal Building in Oklahoma City. The six-story building was almost completely destroyed and 168 people—including 19 children in a day-care center—died. Oklahoma City was a wakeup call to America that our homeland was vulnerable. It also proved that not all terrorists were foreigners. In the years after the bombing, federal and local officials added security and ran drills to learn how to handle a terrorist strike. But America was not prepared for an attack on the scale of September 11th. And no one predicted the methods the terrorists would use to kill so many.

How were the terrorists able to succeed?

AMERICANS HAVE worried about terrorist attacks for several years. The government has prepared for possible attacks, though many critics say it never prepared enough. Federal law enforcement and intelligence agencies have kept a close eye and ear on terrorist leaders, hoping to catch them, or at least find out what they're planning. Many terrorist attacks have been prevented by the Federal Bureau of Investigation (FBI), which investigates crimes, the Central Intelligence Agency (CIA), which gathers top-secret information outside the U.S., and other intelligence agencies. A plot to set off a bomb inside Los Angeles International Airport on New Year's Eve, 2000, was foiled when guards on the U.S.-Canada border found explosives in an Algerian man's car trunk. There were warning signs before September 11th—government agencies intercepted phone calls from known terrorists overseas talking about something big planned for the end of summer. But government officials concluded that American

5:00   6:00   7:00   8:00   ▼ 8:35 A.M.   9:00   10:00   11:00

The Federal Aviation Administration (FAA) alerts the North American Aerospace Defense Command (NORAD) that American Airlines Flight 11 has been hijacked.

embassies in foreign countries were in far more danger than the United States. They never got any more clues. September 11th took everyone by surprise.

Part of the reason no one anticipated the attacks was the way the terrorists struck. Previous terrorist attacks had usually involved bombs. Americans also worried about attacks with biological, chemical, or possibly nuclear weapons. Terrorists like to spread fear, and these weapons inspire the most panic. But while everyone was watching for those attacks, the terrorists hit where no one was looking. Airplane security was not as tight as it should have been. Previous hijackers have usually taken over a plane and made demands to the government, but rarely killed passengers. Pilots were trained to cooperate with hijackers to avoid putting passengers at risk.

Why attack the twin towers and the Pentagon?

THE PENTAGON and World Trade Center are powerful symbols of America. The terrorists imagined that they are part of what defines us. The Pentagon is a symbol of the military strength that has helped make the U.S. the world's only superpower at this point in history. The World Trade Center represented our financial strength. The U.S. economy, the largest in the world, was built by the kind of people who worked in the twin towers. That economy has spread throughout the world—why else would people from eighty nations have been in the Trade Center that day? And the towers themselves were more than concrete, steel, and glass. They were a remarkable achievement, two 110-story skyscrapers

12:00   1:00   2:00   3:00   4:00   5:00   6:00

9/11/01
P.M.

reaching up into the sky itself. To most of the world, their existence was a symbol of what people could accomplish. To the terrorists, they were a symbol of America's arrogance.

The twin towers were meant to symbolize peace. Shortly after they were finished in 1973, the architect who designed them, Japanese-American Minoru Yamasaki, said, "World trade means world peace. The World Trade Center is a living symbol of man's dedication to world peace. It should become a representation of man's belief in humanity, his need for individual dignity, his beliefs in the cooperation of men, and through cooperation, his ability to find greatness." The terrorists were striking at all of this.

They were also trying to spread fear. Terrorists don't only want to kill people, they want to frighten the rest of us into doing what they want. And the towers and the Pentagon were perfect targets for that. By showing they could hit the headquarters of the U.S. military and one of our largest financial centers, they sought to remind us that America is vulnerable. By bringing down two of our tallest buildings, they tried to prove they were stronger than the U.S. And they wanted the entire world to see it. The first plane got everyone's attention, then with the whole world watching, they hit the second tower.

2.
Who were the hijackers?

MOHAMMED ATTA, Abdulaziz al Omari, Satam Suqami, Wail al Shehri, Waleed al Shehri. Hani Hanjour, Khalid al Midhar, Majed Moqed, Nawaf al Hazmi, Salem al Hazmi. Ziad Samir Jarrah, Saeed al Ghamdi, Ahmad al Haznawi, Ahmed al Nami. Marwan al Shehhi, Ahmed al Ghamdi, Fayez Ahmed al Qadi Banihammad, Mohand al Shehri, Hamza al Ghamdi.

Very little is actually known about these nineteen men who killed more than three thousand people. We don't even know if these are their real names—as many as fifteen of them may have used false identities to buy their plane tickets. After the attacks, these were the best guesses the FBI was able to put together from the lists of passengers on the four planes.

We do know that the nineteen men were all terrorists from Middle Eastern nations—Saudi Arabia, Egypt, the United Arab Emirates, and possibly others. Investigators have learned that the nineteen belonged to an international terrorist organization known as al Qaeda, led by a man named Osama bin Laden. He is a well-known terrorist who began a violent campaign against the United States in the early 1990s in an effort to drive U.S. military, business, and government interests out of Islamic countries. Bin Laden and his followers are Muslims, and though their religion preaches peace and tolerance, they have used it to justify the September 11th attacks.

While investigators have linked the hijackers with al Qaeda and bin Laden, they don't know much about their lives before the attacks. Few of the nineteen showed any signs of extremist beliefs. Their parents and friends were shocked to find out they were behind such deadly attacks. Some were known to be devout Muslims, but not terrorists. Others had told their parents when they left home that they were going to fight with other Muslims against Russians in Chechnya, a Russian state where local Muslims have been trying to secede. Ziad Jarrah told his girlfriend before he left his home in Germany, where he was an exchange student, that he was traveling to Afghanistan. But in reality all the young men were heading to America on a suicide mission.

What was Atta's life like before he became a terrorist?

MOHAMMED ATTA is widely believed to have been the terrorists' ringleader. But many of Atta's childhood friends in Egypt find it hard to believe he helped kill thousands of people. They remember him as a shy, sweet boy, who would get upset if someone killed an insect. Atta grew up in a middle-class family in Cairo. His father was a lawyer and his mother was a homemaker. His two sisters were well educated—one became a zoology professor, the other a doctor. Atta himself worked hard in school and graduated from Cairo University with a degree in architectural engineering. He was interested in planning cities.

5:00   6:00   7:00   8:00   9:00   10:00   11:00

▼ 8:42 A.M.

9/11/01

United Airlines Flight 93 to San Francisco departs from Newark Airport in New Jersey with 38 passengers and 7 crew members on board.

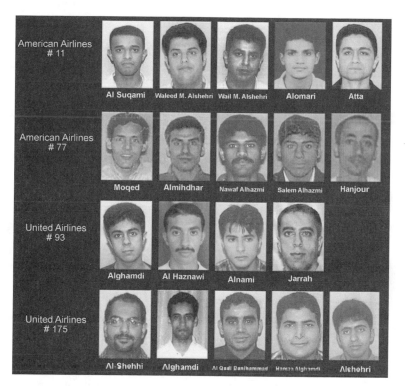

The U.S. Department of Justice released this image identifying the names and faces of the nineteen hijackers just a couple of weeks after the attacks. (Spellings of names vary due to transliteration differences.)

But in 1992, at the age of twenty-four, Atta traveled to Hamburg, Germany, for graduate school, and he slowly began to change. He became more outspoken. He also became more frustrated, complaining to friends that Muslims around the world were being repressed and treated unfairly. He started taking long trips all over the Middle East. He told friends and professors he was doing research for school, but investigators believe he was meeting with al Qaeda members. Finally, in 1997, he disappeared for more than a year. When he came back to Hamburg, no one recognized him. Atta had grown a long bushy beard and become very serious, rarely smiling. He took his Muslim faith much more seriously, beginning an Islamic study group among university students. Over forty young men joined the group, including Marwan al Shehhi and Ziad Jarrah. The group began meeting daily to pray.

In the summer of 2000, Atta and al Shehhi left Hamburg and moved to the United States. They found a place to live in South Florida and began taking lessons at a local flight school. Atta had shaved his beard off by this time. He was on a mission in America, and he wanted to blend in.

How did the hijackers live in America for so long without getting caught?

NO ONE knew the terrorists were living in the U.S. because they had such a simple plan that no one suspected it. Past terrorists have been caught sneaking into the country with explosives or weapons. The hijackers didn't need any. They used small knives that can be bought at any hardware store. They turned our own airplanes into weapons. You don't need explosives when a 767 is packed with 24,000 gallons of jet fuel. Almost none of the hijackers were known terrorists. They easily acquired student or tourist visas to visit the U.S.

They also remained undetected because federal agents looking for possible terrorists often watch for foreigners receiving large amounts of money from overseas. But the hijackers needed little money compared to most terrorists. Their plan was relatively cheap—the entire scheme cost less than a million dollars. When accomplices in Europe wired them cash, it was in small enough quantities—less than $10,000—that no one noticed.

The terrorists arrived in America in scattered groups, most of them

5:00   6:00   7:00   8:00   9:00   10:00   11:00

▼ 8:43 A.M.

9/11/01
A.M.

The FAA notifies NORAD that United Airlines Flight 175 has been hijacked.

during the two years before the attacks. Once in the country, they worked hard not to be noticed. They dressed like average Americans, usually in khaki pants and casual shirts. They had American haircuts—and no long beards. They did not talk about religion and never attended prayers at local mosques. They ate in fast food restaurants and lived in cheap apartments in out-of-the-way neighborhoods, either alone or in small groups with some of the other terrorists. Although no one knows for sure, none of them are believed to have had jobs. They spent all their time preparing for the attacks. Some of them lived in California, some in Arizona, but most lived in Florida. Neighbors noticed them but weren't suspicious—

A Twentieth Hijacker?

ALL FOUR teams of hijackers had five members—except the one on flight 93, the plane that crashed in Pennsylvania. U.S. authorities believe that's because the fifth member was in jail. Federal agents arrested French Muslim Zacarias Moussaoui on August 16, 2001, on immigration charges. He had been training at flight schools in Oklahoma and Minnesota since February and had attracted attention because, although he had never learned to fly small planes well, he kept asking to learn how to fly large passenger jets.

Suspicious of his intentions, instructors called the FBI. Agents questioned him, but never suspected he might be part of a larger plot. They didn't foresee 9/11. Six months after the attacks, the government was preparing to try Moussaoui for conspiring with al Qaeda. He faces the death penalty if convicted.

the young men blended right in. A few of them wrote letters to their families back home, but they never revealed why they were in America.

With its warm sunny weather, Florida is home to many flight schools, and aspiring pilots from all over the world go there to learn to fly. Atta and

A bank's surveillance camera recorded two of the terrorists—Hani Hanjour (left) and Majed Moqed—at an ATM just days before September 11th.

al Shehhi were just two of many foreign students taking classes at Huffman Aviation International in Venice, Florida, in June of 2000. Instructors remember Atta as cold and unfriendly but say al Shehhi was talkative and funny. By December, Atta and al Shehhi had their pilot licenses. The remaining hijackers who learned to fly took lessons at other schools in much the same fashion. Several of the pilots bought Global Positioning System (GPS) devices, which could be used onboard a plane to help navigate. It would be easy for even an inexperienced pilot to use them to chart a path straight into the twin towers. The terrorists who didn't take flight lessons joined local gyms or took martial arts classes to make sure they could physically control the passengers during the attacks.

Atta traveled extensively in 2001, while the scattered groups of hijackers continued to train. Investigators know he traveled to Spain twice but are unsure whom he met with. In the months after September 11th, Spanish police arrested more than a dozen men believed to be al Qaeda members. The hijackers, especially Atta, also carefully scouted the routes for their attacks. They took the exact same flights they would take on the 11th to see how crowded the flights generally were.

During the week of September 6th, the hijackers traveled to Boston; Portland, Maine; Newark; and Washington, forming four separate groups.

5:00   6:00   7:00   8:00   9:00   10:00   11:00

▼ 8:44 A.M.

Two F-15 fighter jets from Otis Air National Guard Base in Falmouth, Massachusetts, take off and head toward New York City.

On the morning of the 11th, Atta and Abdulaziz al Omari walked through the Portland airport's security checkpoint, looking like any other travelers. An American Airlines agent at Dulles Airport in Washington D.C. helped Nawaf al Hazmi and Salem al Hazmi check in for flight 77. She found it odd they had expensive first-class tickets but were standing in the line for coach, but they showed her valid IDs and boarded without a problem.

What were the terrorists thinking?

THE NINETEEN hijackers lived a double life. They blended into normal American neighborhoods and lived seemingly ordinary lives. They walked among us for two years yet did not hesitate to kill thousands of us. In fact, it was what they were working toward the entire time.

They were motivated by a very powerful faith—their extremist interpretation of Islam. Al Qaeda has taken one of the world's major religions and twisted its teachings to justify mass murder. Osama bin Laden has told his followers that God wants his faithful to kill Americans no matter what the cost. Al Qaeda members believe whoever dies attacking America will be rewarded with an eternity in paradise. To Mohammed Atta and his partners, this attack was not suicide. It was serving God.

Identical copies of an anonymous letter written in Arabic were found in Atta's luggage, in another hijacker's rental car, and in the wreckage of flight 93. Part of it reads, "Purify your heart and forget something called life, for the time of play is gone and the time of truth has come. . . . When the plane starts moving, then you are traveling toward God and what a blessing that travel is."

3.
What is terrorism?

AN EXPLOSION SHOOK an abortion clinic in Atlanta, Georgia, on the morning of January 16, 1997. No one was hurt, but police and journalists rushed to the scene. Then a second bomb went off, injuring six people, including police officers, rescue workers, and a TV cameraman. The second explosion was seen on TV all over America that day. On August 15, 1998, police in Omagh, Northern Ireland, received a mysterious phone call. Someone told them a bomb was about to explode in the town market. Before the police could clear the market, a car bomb exploded, killing twenty-eight people and wounding almost two hundred. On August 9, 2001, in Jerusalem, Israel, a Palestinian man walked up to a crowded pizzeria and detonated a bomb strapped to his chest. The explosion killed fifteen other people, including one American.

These three bombings took place on different days on opposite sides of the globe. The attackers had little in common except that they were all terrorists. But what does that mean? What is terrorism? It can be as hard to define as it is to understand. All three of these violent acts seem random and senseless, but in each case, the terrorists had a planned goal. They hoped to frighten their enemies into giving them what they wanted.

5:00　6:00　7:00　8:00　9:00　10:00　11:00

Terrorists commit violence to make people afraid.

America was flooded with fear after September 11th. People did not know if the terrorists would strike again, where they would attack or how. Travelers were afraid to fly. There were reports of suspicious people near water reservoirs, on trains, outside power plants. Americans worried the next attack could involve biological weapons spreading diseases such as anthrax or smallpox. When threatening letters filled with anthrax turned up in Florida, New York, and Washington D.C. just weeks after the attacks, the fears seemed justified. Desperate to protect themselves, some people rushed to buy gas masks and powerful antibiotics. It was impossible not to be afraid.

Terrorists don't believe they are doing anything wrong. They are political dissidents—people who disagree with a government and are trying to force that government to change its policies. They don't have the money or power or influence to fight their enemies in a war, so random violence and the death of innocent people are justified in their eyes. In 1894, French terrorist Emile Henry threw a homemade bomb into a Paris café. At his trial, the judge asked why Henry attacked innocent people. Henry replied, "There are no innocent."

Terrorists will use any method they can, as long as it spreads fear and draws attention to their cause. Terrorists have assassinated political leaders, used bombs to kill innocents, set fires, hijacked planes, and kidnapped people. A terrorist group in Chile once claimed to have put cyanide in grapes. It is impossible for the world to predict and prevent all these attacks, and this empowers the terrorists. Once the world is paying attention to them, the terrorists hope that some people will begin to sympathize with their cause and pressure their enemies to give in. If that doesn't work, there is always the threat of more violence.

12:00   1:00   2:00   3:00   4:00   5:00   6:00

Has terrorism existed for a long time?

ONE OF the first recorded terrorist campaigns took place in the first century, in ancient Israel, which at that time was ruled by the Romans. A Jewish political party called the Zealots wanted to liberate their country, and its members believed violent revolt was the only method that would work. Members of the party called Biryonim would stab Roman officials with long daggers, usually in bustling markets where they could escape into the crowd. Their goal was to create an environment of fear—to make the Romans feel so unsafe they would abandon the country.

The Biryonim were not that different from modern terrorists. But one thing has changed in the last hundred years. Before the twentieth century, terrorists tended to focus their attacks on political leaders. Now, innocent civilians are often their targets. Remember, until the twentieth century, most of the world was ruled by kings—America being a notable exception. Terrorists could assassinate the king to show their power and force political change. (The word "assassin" actually comes from the name of a Middle Eastern terrorist group from the twelfth century). But nowadays, there aren't many countries run by kings. And even those usually have large governments made up of many officials. Assassination has become a far less effective tool than random attacks on civilians. The horror of seeing innocent people kidnapped or killed has been enough to force many governments to give in to terrorist demands, or at least to negotiate.

Another aspect of terrorism that has changed in the last hundred years is its international nature. The world is a smaller place now—we can

5:00   6:00   7:00   8:00   9:00   10:00   11:00

▼ 8:47 A.M.

American Airlines Flight 11 crashes into the north tower of the World Trade Center in New York. It is carrying 24,000 gallons of jet fuel and destroys floors 90 through 100.

watch what's happening on the other side of the globe, or travel there in just a few hours. Terrorism used to be a crime that only affected the country where it took place. Now the whole world watches when terrorists strike. And often, the whole world gets involved. There are two places in particular where terrorism has grabbed the world's attention in recent times—Israel and Northern Ireland. Looking at these conflicts might help us understand why someone would turn to terror.

What do terrorists in Israel and Northern Ireland hope to accomplish?

PALESTINIAN GROUPS have been using terrorism for thirty-five years in their struggle with Israelis. But the region has long been torn by violence—Jewish groups conducted a series of terrorist attacks in the first half of the twentieth century. At that time, Israel was called Palestine and was part of the Ottoman Empire. It became a British colony in 1919. European Jews had been immigrating there for several decades. The Palestinians did not welcome them. They did not want Jews in their territory. Followers of a Jewish movement called Zionism believed that they needed to create a new homeland in Palestine. They mounted terrorist attacks on the British and the Palestinians. The Palestinians also attacked the British.

At the end of World War II, in 1945, Great Britain withdrew from Palestine, and the United Nations voted to give half of the land to the Jews, creating the new nation of Israel. The Palestinians and nearby Muslim nations were upset and rejected the U.N. proposal. They invaded Israel several times. In 1967, Israel occupied the land that the United Nations

12:00   1:00   2:00   3:00   4:00   5:00   6:00

9/11/01
P.M

A mother grieves at the funeral of her son, one of the Israeli athletes murdered by Palestinian terrorists during the Munich Olympics in 1972.

had left to the Palestinians. Soon afterward, Palestinian terrorist groups began attacking Israel and its allies. In 1968, the Popular Front for the Liberation of Palestine launched the first in a series of hijackings, forcing pilots at gunpoint to fly an Israeli commercial plane to Algeria. In 1972, another group, Black September, murdered eleven Israeli athletes at the Summer Olympics in Munich.

Some of these groups hoped to frighten the Israelis into ending their occupation of Palestinian lands. Others never accepted Israel's right to exist at all—they want all of Israel to belong to Palestinians. All of the terrorist groups have succeeded in bringing international attention to their cause. With American support, Israel and the Palestinian Liberation

5:00   6:00   7:00   8:00   9:00   ▼ 9:00 A.M.   10:00   11:00

9/11/01
A.M.
President Bush arrives at a school in Sarasota, Florida, and is told that a plane has crashed into the World Trade Center.

attacks on the Protestants and the British soldiers who policed the province—bombings, killings, and other random violence. Protestant terrorist groups attacked Catholics as well. Even America became involved, as Irish Americans sent financial aid—and sometimes guns—to the IRA and other Catholic groups.

The dispute between these groups seemed unstoppable. To many Catholics, the Protestants were foreign invaders representing continued British rule. But the Protestants saw themselves as lawful citizens whose families have lived in Ireland for hundreds of years. Religion and nationality divided them. But there is new hope in Northern Ireland. In 1998, with American and English help, the Protestants and Catholics formed a unified government, which has ruled Ulster ever since. That government has faced struggles, and small terrorist groups on both sides continue to launch isolated attacks—the bombing in Omagh was carried out by such a group. The tension between these two peoples won't disappear overnight, but the people of Ulster have put aside violence for now.

What role does religion play in terrorism?

TERRORISM HAS usually had nationalist or political motives. In both Israel and Northern Ireland, the combatants are divided by different religions, but the terrorists fight for political goals. Both the PLO and the IRA want their own state. But terrorists have begun to fight more for religious reasons lately. And when religion motivates violence, it can be very dangerous. Political terrorists believe they are fighting for a just cause. Religious terrorists believe they are fighting for God.

Americans in the Middle East were suddenly the target of attacks by militantly religious terrorists in the early 1980s. Lebanon was torn by a civil war at that time, and religious terrorists did much of the fighting. A group called Hezbollah, which is Arabic for "Party of God," kidnapped Americans and held them hostage, and bombed the U.S. Marines barracks in Beirut, Lebanon, in 1983, killing 241 soldiers. Hezbollah was receiving money and support from Iran. The Muslim leaders who governed Iran wanted to spread their revolutionary ideals; they wanted strict Islamist governments to take over other nations in the Middle East such as Lebanon. An Islamist government rules by the laws of Islam. Hezbollah and other religious terrorists helped Iran's leaders spread these ideals.

In 1979, the Soviet Union invaded the Muslim country of Afghanistan. This South Asian country was ruled by an unpopular communist government, and the Soviets came to help keep it in power. But the Afghans grew incensed over this foreign occupation. They fought back and appealed to their Muslim brethren throughout the world to help them. Many young Muslims from across the Middle East came to their aid. These same men would later return to their home countries filled with a sense of a common bond.

What began in Iran and Afghanistan had profound effects on terrorism in the final years of the twentieth century. The world had entered a new period of globalization where people from many nations were closer than ever before, thanks to new technology allowing instant communication and faster travel. The young Muslims who had met in Afghanistan suddenly had ties to like-minded revolutionaries in many different countries. One group founded in the battles of Afghanistan was al Qaeda, the organization that attacked America on September 11th, the group founded by Osama bin Laden.

5:00   6:00   7:00   8:00   9:00   ▼ 9:05 A.M.   10:00   11:00

9/11/01
A.M.   The president is told another airplane has struck the twin towers.

What makes al Qaeda different from other terrorist groups?

AL QAEDA represents a dramatic change in terrorism. Terrorists are usually motivated by local issues. Palestinian groups are fighting for a homeland. The IRA used terror to try to gain independence. But al Qaeda has members in over sixty different nations. It is pan-Islamic, uniting Muslims from throughout the world in a common cause. Its goal is to force America to stay out of Middle Eastern affairs and withdraw our military from the region. It also wants to overthrow any government in a Muslim country that does not rule by what it believes are Islamic principles. It even hopes to form a new Muslim empire.

During the 1990s the number of terrorist attacks worldwide declined, but the average number of people killed in each attack rose dramatically. Before September 11th, there had been only fourteen terrorist attacks ever with more than a hundred fatalities. Throughout history, terrorists have been careful to limit how much violence they use. Mass murder could so horrify people it would actually weaken their cause. But al Qaeda is motivated purely by religion. Its members believe they are in a holy struggle between good and evil. And when you believe God is on your side, mass murder becomes acceptable. These terrorists believe it is in fact commanded by God. Al Qaeda's leaders may hope that by targeting America with such deadly tactics, they can inspire Muslims everywhere to fight against America.

With so many members in so many countries, al Qaeda has been able to plan terrorist attacks on a larger scale than any previous group. In

12:00 1:00 2:00 3:00 4:00 5:00 6:00

The Encyclopedia of Jihad

ONE KEY to al Qaeda's success as a terrorist organization is its international nature. With members in more than sixty countries, Osama bin Laden's network of terrorists can share all their knowledge and experience. They often use the internet to swap ideas and intelligence. And their leaders have compiled their terrorist knowledge in what may be the world's most frightening book—*The Encyclopedia of Jihad*. The Arabic word *jihad* means holy war, and this eleven-volume encyclopedia explains all the different methods of waging a terrorist war. The encyclopedia is six thousand pages long and many al Qaeda members carry it on CD-ROM.

SOME OF THE INFORMATION IN IT:

- How to booby-trap a door, a radio, a TV, or a couch.
- How to find and use explosive chemicals for bombs.
- How to inject toxic gas into an office building's air conditioning system.
- How to blend in while living in America or Europe.
- In its deadliest chapter, how to use biological weapons.

1998, al Qaeda terrorists blew up truck bombs outside U.S. embassies in Kenya and Uganda, killing 224 people. In late 1999, several members were caught planning to attack Los Angeles International Airport and several hotels in Jordan during the millennium celebrations on New Year's Eve. In October of 2000, al Qaeda operatives blew up a bomb on a small boat approaching the U.S.S. *Cole*, a naval ship visiting Yemen. And eleven months later, al Qaeda attacked New York and Washington D.C. Investigators have learned that most, if not all, of these operations took at least four years to plan. That means al Qaeda was planning them simultaneously. There may be more still in the planning stages. No other terror-

5:00 6:00 7:00 8:00 9:00 10:00 11:00

▼ 9:09 A.M.

9/11/01

New York City mayor Rudolf Giuliani races to the fire command post in the World Trade Center.

ist group has ever planned so big, operated in so many countries, or killed so many people at once.

The United States now faces fighting not only al Qaeda's leadership, but its scattered groups of terrorists, or cells, throughout the world. And there is much concern about terrorism's future. Will groups continue to use increasingly deadly tactics, including attacks with biological, chemical, or nuclear weapons? The ability of a small group of people to threaten the entire world with mass murder is a powerful weapon. Preventing such attacks is crucial. The world was caught asleep on September 11th. Understanding terrorists' motives, no matter how misguided, can help stop them. Intelligence agencies like the CIA or the Defense Intelligence Agency (DIA) can gather information about terrorists and better predict where they will strike next. And if our government and others work to end international grievances and violent disputes—like the conflicts in Israel and Northern Ireland—we can try to bring peace before the violence gets out of hand.

4.
What is Islam?

ONCE A YEAR, the Saudi Arabian city of Mecca is flooded with more than two million visitors. They arrive from dozens of countries around the world. Some check into luxurious hotel rooms while others pitch tents. But soon afterward they all put on white robes and walk to a vast court-yard larger than a football field. Tens of thousands of the visitors begin to circle a rectangular shrine in the center, chanting and praying. This is the beginning of four days of rituals and prayers, and these two million visi-tors, no matter where they come from or what language they speak or how much money they have, will spend the next four days as equals, bound by a common faith. These are Muslims, people who believe in the religion of Islam, and they are all pilgrims—making a once-in-a-lifetime journey to their holy city. They are all connected by their belief in one God, and in the religion Islam.

The terrorists who attacked America on September 11th justified their actions by claiming they were killing for Islam. Osama bin Laden thanked Allah, Arabic for God or the One, for the success of the attacks. But most Muslims were horrified by what happened on September 11th. How could a religion that preaches peace and tolerance be used to justify the murder of thousands of people? Understanding Islam, and how it could be hijacked like a plane and used as an excuse for mass murder, is key to understanding September 11th.

What is Islam?

ISLAM IS one of the world's largest religions, with more than one billion believers. It was begun by the prophet Muhammad, who lived and preached in Arabia, in what is now Saudi Arabia in the heart of the Middle East, in the early seventh century A.D. Although Islam originated in the Middle East, it has found converts everywhere. The three largest Muslim populations are in Indonesia, Pakistan, and India, far outside the Middle East. Islam is the second largest religion in France, behind only Catholicism. Of the 278 million people living in the United States, about 6 million are Muslim, 5.6 million are Jewish, and 234 million are Christian. Some of the Muslims are recent immigrants from the Middle East and other Muslim countries, but others come from families who have lived in the United States for generations, some of whom have decided to convert to Islam only recently.

Islam is closely related to two other religions born in the Middle East—Christianity and Judaism. Muhammad believed that he was following in the footsteps of Moses and Jesus as a prophet—someone who believes he speaks for God, bringing a divine message to the world. And though they have had sharp disagreements for centuries, Jews, Christians and Muslims still have much in common. Like Jews and Christians, Muslims believe in one God, and believe that God judges their actions on earth. And they interpret the teachings of their religion in many different ways. Not all believe in the exact same teachings—they often disagree on what their religion means. And though Islam preaches peace and tolerance, some Muslims, just like some Jews and Christians, have used their religion to justify violence against people of different faiths.

What do Muslims believe?

ISLAM IS an Arabic word meaning surrender. All someone has to do to become a Muslim is surrender to God—accept that there is one God, who gave him life and a soul and watches over everything he does, and that Muhammad was a prophet of God. This profession of faith is called the *shahada*. And it is the first of the five pillars of belief in Islam.

The other pillars are prayer, charity, fasting, and pilgrimage. Muslims pray five times a day to God—at dawn, midday, midafternoon, evening, and night. They stop whatever they are doing, calm their thoughts, and begin to chant prayers. Muslims can pray alone or in a group. They try to pray together in a mosque, a house of worship similar to a church, at least once a week, at midday on Friday, their Sabbath. They form even lines and bow toward Mecca, the city where Muhammad first began to preach. There is no priest to lead them. In fact, there are no priests of any kind in Islam. Particularly learned Muslims, called mullahs, give sermons at Friday midday services. Although they are not considered leaders, many Muslims ask their advice. One of Islam's most important teachings is that no one stands between a believer and God. And Muslims worship no one other than God, not even Muhammad. There are no saints in Islam. Inside the mosque, there are no stained-glass windows or paintings of Allah or Muhammad or anyone else. Allah's appearance is a mystery. And any portrait of man or

5:00   6:00   7:00   8:00   9:00   10:00   11:00

▼ 9:21 A.M.

9/11/01   The Port Authority of New York and New Jersey orders that all bridges and tunnels in the metropolitan area be closed.

animal in the mosque would be considered idolatry—worshipping someone other than God. Mosques are usually decorated with verses from the Qur'an, the holy book of Islam.

The third pillar is charity. Helping the needy is very important to Muslims. In fact, many Muslim countries require citizens to pay a *zakat*, a charitable donation that goes to help the poor. Muslim charities operate throughout the world so that Muslims can give regularly. Charity reminds Muslims to be compassionate. It also reminds them that material goods do not matter in the long run. They believe that God judges them on their actions, not on how much money they have.

Thousands of Muslims gather to pray at al Haram, the great mosque in the holy city of Mecca.

The fourth pillar is fasting. During the month of Ramadan, Muslims do not eat or drink from sunrise to sunset. After the sun sets, families gather to pray and eat a feast. Although twenty-eight days of fasting is not easy, Muslims believe it teaches discipline. You learn to forget about material things like food and to focus on God.

The final pillar is the *hajj*—the pilgrimage to Mecca. This four-day

journey retraces the steps of Abraham. The biblical patriarch was the first Jew, but Muslims and Christians as well see him as the father of monotheism, the belief in one God. While Jews believe they are descended from Abraham's son Isaac, Muslims believe they are descendants of his older son, Ishmael. All Muslims are expected to journey to Mecca once during their lifetimes, to walk where they believe Abraham, Ishmael, and Muhammad all walked. The process shows them how strong their faith is and how Islam attracts people from all over the world, and reminds them that they are all equal in God's eyes.

Who was Muhammad?

IN THE year A.D. 610, Arabia was a backward place. Two great empires, Rome and Persia, controlled large swaths of territory in the Middle East. Arabia was off the beaten path, a land of fierce nomadic tribes called Bedouins and isolated towns of merchants and their families. But in less than one hundred years, the Arabians had united under a new religion, Islam, and formed a vast empire of their own, by conquests that stretched from Spain to India. Muhammad was their prophet, the man who brought them Islam.

Little is known about Muhammad. He was born around 570 to a merchant family in Mecca, in what is now Saudi Arabia. Mecca was already a holy place to Arabians. In the center of town was the Kabah, a square where the Arabians would place their idols of the various gods they worshipped. Muhammad's father died before he was born and his mother died when he was six; so as a boy he was raised by relatives. He became a merchant and married. And then, at roughly forty years old, his life changed dramatically.

5:00   6:00   7:00   8:00   9:00   10:00   11:00

▼ 9:24 A.M.

9/11/01
A M   The FAA notifies NORAD that American Airlines Flight 77 has been hijacked.

According to the Qur'an, Islam's holy book, on a starry night in the year 610, Muhammad climbed to a cave on top of Mount Hira, outside of Mecca, where he would sometimes meditate. The angel Gabriel appeared before him and began to declare the word of God to Muhammad. "Recite," he said.

Muhammad replied, "What should I recite?"

"Recite in the name of your Lord."

Muhammad began to preach to any Meccan who would listen that there was only one God and that they must abandon their idols and seek God's forgiveness or face damnation in the afterlife. Within twenty-two years, virtually all of Arabia had converted to this religion he preached. But for the first twelve, he had little luck. He found few converts. The town elders, the wealthiest traders, mistrusted him. He was preaching that all men were equal in the eyes of God, which didn't sound like such a good idea to the men who ruled over the city. So in 622, when the nearby city of Yathrib invited Muhammad to bring his Muslims to their city, he eagerly left with his small band of followers. Soon afterward, the people made him leader of the city, which they renamed Medinat al Rasul, City of the Messenger. Today it is known as Medina. As leader, Muhammad became judge and lawgiver. His preachings began to focus on how members of the community of Muslims, the *umma*, should treat each other. As the umma grew, old tribal affiliations began to matter less.

As Muhammad won more and more converts to Islam, the leaders in Mecca decided to attack his people. The two cities were locked in war until 630, when the Muslims defeated Mecca and took over the city. Muhammad and his followers destroyed all the idols around the Kabah and dedicated the site to Allah. Soon all the people of Arabia began to view Muhammad as their leader. But the prophet's time was nearing an end. He died in 632.

What are Islamic beliefs

TO WESTERN observers, the treatment of women in Islamic countries often seems backward. The images of women wearing veils or being denied the same rights as men can be upsetting. But is Islam itself to blame? The faith does treat women differently on some matters. But often rules concerning women in Islamic countries owe more to local customs than to religious beliefs.

In seventh-century Arabia, Muhammad actually improved life for women—at that time, women's status could only get better. Baby girls were sometimes buried alive in the desert, unwanted by families that prized boys. Women had few rights of any kind. Muhammad gave them some rights. Under Islam, women were finally allowed to inherit money and property from relatives. Women were made full participants in the religion and were expected to obey all five of the pillars of faith. Women pray in the same mosques as men today, though often they must do so in separate rooms, and they too must make the pilgrimage to Mecca. Women have the same opportunity as men to enter paradise when they die.

But in societal matters in Muhammad's Arabia, Islam largely maintained the status quo. Men were expected to be the leaders. The Qur'an says, "Men have authority over women because Allah has made the one superior to the others. . . . Good women are obedient." And women were expected to be modest, to cover themselves in front of strangers, and to be obedient to their husbands.

In some ways, life for Muslim women has improved today, but in others it has not. Men in Saudi Arabia are still allowed to have four wives, as they did in Muhammad's time, and none of those wives are allowed to drive a car or travel without their husband's permission. Although in Islamic nations in Asia, women have much the same rights as men, in some Middle Eastern countries, women cannot work in the same room as men or be in the same room in public places such as banks. Men in those nations where women continue to be oppressed often use Islam to justify their backward cultural beliefs. But different Muslim nations have different

Two F-16 fighter jets from Langley Air Force Base in Virginia take off, heading for the Washington D.C. area.

toward women?

rules for women, based on local traditions. All you need to do to understand this is to look at women's dress in various Muslim nations. In Afghanistan, even after the Taliban, some women continue to wear *burqas*–the full-length shrouds that the Taliban mandated. It's what their mothers did. In Saudi Arabia, they wear the *hijab*, a head scarf and veil that covers the face. In Iran and many other Islamic states, women simply cover most of their hair with a scarf. In Turkey, most women don't even wear scarves. In fact, the government has forbidden scarf wearing in public buildings, including universities. Some women have protested for the right to wear them.

After the departure of the Taliban, an Afghan woman lifts her *burqa* and shyly reveals part of her face.

Conservative attitudes toward women are not a uniquely Muslim phenomenon. Until the early twentieth century, women could not vote in the United States and most of Europe. And while American ladies' hair went uncovered, if one of them showed her ankles it was a scandal. In an ideal world there would be no sexism. But is it insensitive to force other countries to accept our notions of women's rights? Groups in the United States have tried to do just that by urging our government not to give financial aid or even recognize countries diplomatically that do not end strict restrictions on women. Will treating these countries as outcasts make them change their practices toward women? There's no easy answer, but learning about other cultures is the only way to understand them.

What is the Qur'an?

THE QUR'AN, or Koran, is the holy book of Islam. Muslims believe that the original Qur'an is in heaven, and that God recited its words to Muhammad, who repeated them to his followers. Muslims do not believe Muhammad wrote the book; in fact, the prophet was illiterate. But some of his followers wrote his recitations down and brought them together in one book shortly after he died.

To Muslims, the Qur'an is sacred, the source of their beliefs and proof of God's wisdom. Muslim prayer consists of reciting the Arabic verses that make up the book. Religious schools begin teaching the book to students at an early age. They learn to recite the passages by heart. In fact, it is a mark of pride for a Muslim to be able to recite the entire Qur'an from memory—that's more than 77,000 words, almost three times as long as this book. Many read from it every day. While all Muslims pray in the original Arabic, the book has been translated into dozens of languages including English, so that all Muslims can read and understand what the book teaches.

The Qur'an is not just a book about faith. Its teachings cover many different aspects of life. The chapters from Muhammad's early days in Mecca speak of God and Judgment Day and heaven. But the later chapters, or *suras*, from when Muhammad ruled Medina, talk of how Muslims should treat each other in daily life. They speak of rules for business, for love, for marriage. The suras also instruct on government and law.

While the Qur'an is the only divine book of Islam, there are several other important texts. Chief among these are the *hadith*. These writings

5:00   6:00   7:00   8:00   9:00   10:00   11:00

▼ 9:26 A.M.

9/11/01   For the first time ever, the FAA orders all nonmilitary planes grounded and cancels all flights in the U.S.

are believed to be sayings of Muhammad. Even though Muslims do not regard the prophet as a saint, they believe he lived such a good and holy life that all Muslims should see him as a role model. The hadith govern many of the ordinary matters of daily life, from how to conduct business to how to discipline children. In the decades after Muhammad's death, his followers combined the teachings of the Qur'an and the hadith to define the *sunna*—the way or path of Muhammad. To many, there is no better way to live a Muslim life than to follow Muhammad's path. Islamic governments also began to use the sunna as a model for a system of law. Some Muslim goverments today enforce certain rules of *sharia*, or Islamic law. This is a foreign concept to those of us who live in the West where religion and government are meant to stay far apart. But many Muslims believe that their faith governs every aspect of life. After all, Muhammad was both a political and a religious leader to his people.

One of the many conflicts in the modern Muslim world is deciding how much control Islam should have over law, government, and daily life. Some Muslims are Islamists, which means they believe Islam should be the basis of government and law. Islamists want their nations' laws to be based on sharia, ensuring that all citizens are required to obey Muhammad's teachings.

How did Islam build an empire?

MUHAMMAD'S DEATH not only left the Arabs without a prophet, it left them without a leader. His closest advisers decided one of them would have to take his place as political leader. No one could replace him spiritually—Muhammad was the final prophet—but his successor became the caliph, a guardian of the faith. Arabia, long divided by tribal warfare, had united under Islam just as the Roman and Persian empires were weakening. The Arabians saw an opportunity to gain more land, and they took it. They launched raids and invasions. Within seventy years, they had conquered land from Persia (now Iran) to Spain.

This incredible new empire spread the faith of Islam wherever it went. Muslims did not believe in forcibly converting anyone. Christians, Jews,

The Early Spread of Islam

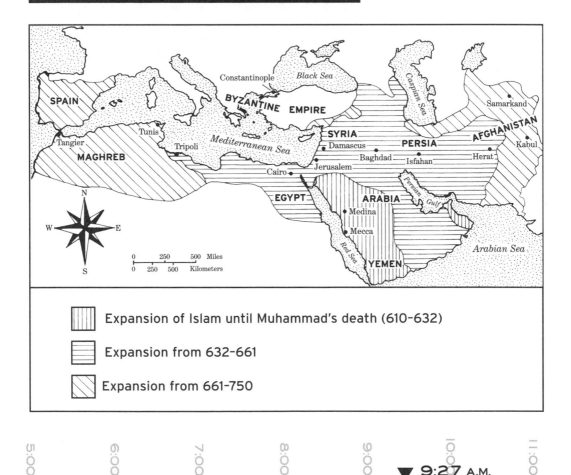

||| Expansion of Islam until Muhammad's death (610-632)

≡ Expansion from 632-661

⫽ Expansion from 661-750

and pagans—people who believe in many gods—who were conquered by Muslims were free to worship whomever they wished. But Muslim citizens did have more rights than their neighbors. And Islam was an appealing faith to many of the people in these new lands. In a time when the social class or tribe you belonged to defined who you were and how you were treated, Islam taught that all people were equal before God, from the caliph to the lowliest soldier. Many people of the Muslims' new lands had been treated as second-class citizens by their previous rulers. The Muslims treated them more fairly. And many people felt disconnected from their faiths. Islam taught that religion was a personal relationship between each person and God, with no priests or other go-betweens. Before long, the faith won many new converts.

As the religion of the Arabs won over people in new lands, the many cultures began to merge. Arabs brought their faith and cultural beliefs to their new homes; the people they conquered brought their own ideas to the mix. These subtly shaped Islam, adding beliefs and practices to what was a relatively new faith. This helped cause several splits in Islam today. Just as Jews and Christians have numerous interpretations of their faiths, from reform to orthodox Judaism and from Catholicism to Quakerism, various groups of Muslims developed different beliefs. Most Muslims believe in the original Sunni teachings. Some of the other major groups are Shi'ites, Sufis, and Wahhabbis. The Shi'ites believe that all Muslims should be governed by descendants of Muhammad. In 656, his cousin Ali became caliph. When a regional official assassinated Ali and made himself caliph, the Shi'ites resisted his authority. The group flourished in Persia and was influenced by earlier Persian beliefs. Modern Iran is ruled by Shi'ite clerics. Sufism is a more mystical Islam, filled with music and dancing as worshippers try to find a more emotional connection to God. Wahhabbism is an attempt to return to the basic beliefs of Islam, stripping away the interpretations and traditions that have developed over more than a millennium to focus again on God, Muhammad, and the Qur'an. This movement developed in the Najd region of Arabia, where the current Saudi rulers live, and much of that nation now follows its teachings.

Despite the many voices the various conquered peoples brought to Islam, it remained a faith where all people are supposed to be treated as equals, no matter what their language or nationality. And because so many nationalities lived in this new Muslim empire, Islam became the glue that held them together. It was their common bond. Much as people from a multitude of cultures live together in the United States bound by a common belief in democracy, Muslims of the great Islamic empires, which lasted in one form or another from the seventh century until 1919, were connected by their religion.

What is jihad?

TO THOSE of us in the West, the stereotype is familiar—Islam is a religion of violence, where suicide bombers and mad warriors kill in the name of God. Certainly hearing the words of Osama bin Laden, who believes God gave him visions of planes hitting tall office buildings, it's believable that Islam has become justification for murder. The jihad, or holy war, has become almost synonymous with Islam. But the Arabic word *jihad* does not literally mean holy war—it means striving for your faith. That can mean war, or it can mean an individual's inner struggle to find his religion and his connection to God. As one American Muslim scholar said, getting out of bed for prayers at dawn is jihad.

5:00 6:00 7:00 8:00 9:00 10:00 11:00

▼ 9:30 A.M.

9/11/01   The president delivers his first official remarks on the attacks from Sarasota, Florida.

Because Muhammad and his followers were attacked repeatedly by the Meccans during the early years of Islam, they often had to fight to defend themselves. Arabia was not a peaceful place at that time. Muhammad himself led his men into battle. And the Qur'an reflects this by saying it is a duty of Muslims to defend their faith if it is challenged. In return, it promises paradise in the afterlife to those who die fighting for Allah. The Qur'an says that those unwilling to struggle for Islam do not really believe in the faith God gave them.

Of course, Muslims have long held different opinions about whether their faith is being challenged. And that is where the concept of jihad has developed its modern meaning of an almost constant holy war against non-believers. Many Muslims believe the West is to blame for the poor quality of life in many Islamic countries today. Some feel the Christians and Jews of Western nations are specifically trying to destroy Islam. To those Muslims who feel the West has mistreated Islam, the only solution seems to be to fight back in defense of the faith. To young Middle Eastern men whose own lives are miserable, dying for God and earning eternity in paradise can sound good. And terrorist leaders like Osama bin Laden are willing to turn those young men into human missiles.

Muslims are not the only believers to kill for their faith. In 1095, when Muslims ruled a mighty empire where people of many religions lived peaceably, Christian Europe was stuck in a dark age. The tiny nations of Europe were trapped in poverty, education was almost nonexistent, and war was constant. Pope Urban II called for a crusade, a holy mission, against the infidels in the Middle East, the Muslims who denied Jesus was the Lord. The pope and other Christians felt it was an insult to Christ that Muslims ruled the lands where Christ had lived and preached. Knights of Europe traveled to Palestine in the first of eight vain attempts to drive all

Muslims from the Holy Land. Those who went were promised eternal bliss in Heaven. Sound familiar?

The Qur'an is filled with passages preaching nonviolence toward both Muslims and non-Muslims. It does justify war in certain cases, but condemns the killing of innocents. While the Qur'an speaks of Muhammad's jihad against his enemies in Mecca, the prophet told his followers the most important jihad was the one a man waged inside— for his own soul. The fact that some Muslims have killed in rage and said they were doing it for God does not make Islam an inherently violent religion. People have long used religion as justification for their violent acts. Is Islam violent? No more than any other religion.

5.
Why does the Middle East matter to us?

IF YOU watch the news, you might think the Middle East is a horrible place. It seems all we hear about the region involves violence or terrorism or suffering. In reality, the Middle East is no more violent than many places in this world. The majority of people there are peaceful and kind. But tragic events there always seem to draw our attention. Part of our concern with the Middle East is religious—it is the birthplace of three of the world's major religions, and many who belong to those faiths passionately care about what goes on there. It is holy ground to them. Part of our concern is economic—the region is home to much of the world's oil, and we depend on that oil for our energy. It keeps our economy going (not to mention all the cars we drive). Part of it is political. Many Middle Eastern countries are politically unstable. Ordinary people there face difficult lives filled with poverty and repression. While those people remain unhappy, terrorists like Osama bin Laden can urge them to turn their unhappiness into anger and aim it at America.

12:00   1:00   2:00   3:00   4:00   5:00   6:00

The Middle East matters because of religion.

THE MIDDLE East is called the Holy Land for a reason. You cannot travel far there without thinking of religion. Judaism, Christianity, and Islam— all three were born there. The cities of the Old Testament, the Gospels, and the Qur'an are all there—Jerusalem, Bethlehem, and Mecca. People from all over the world make pilgrimages to pray at the holy sites of their faith. Because so many people view this land as sacred, they passionately care about what happens there. That can lead to tension and anger between different religious groups and even to violence.

The city that best illustrates this tension is Jerusalem. This city is sacred to all three faiths. To Jews, Jerusalem was the capital of the ancient country of Israel. It was home to the first and second Temples— each the most sacred shrine in Judaism before it was destroyed. To Christians, Jerusalem is where Jesus Christ preached during the finals day of his life—they believe he died on the cross here. The city is sacred to Muslims, too, because they believe Muhammad followed in the foot- steps of the Jewish prophets and Jesus. There is also a traditional story that Muhammad came to the city one night in a dream sent by God and began an ascent into heaven where he met the Lord and all the prophets of history. The spot where Muslims believe he rose into heaven is marked by the Mosque of al Aqsa—the Dome of the Rock. Many Muslims come to pray there. But the land it sits on, the Temple Mount, is also where Jews believe the Temples stood. The one remaining wall of the Second Temple is a short distance away from the mosque, and Jews come there from all

5:00   6:00   7:00   8:00   9:00   ▼ 9:30 A.M.   10:00   11:00

9/11/01
A M   The New York Stock Exchange is evacuated; trading is suspended.

over the world to pray.

The city of Jerusalem is divided today. Part of it is home to Jewish Israelis. Part of it is home to Muslim Palestinians. Because both believe the city belongs to their faith, they have frequently attacked each other for more than forty years. Palestinian snipers have shot into Jewish neighborhoods, hitting innocent Israelis in their homes. Palestinian suicide bombers have blown themselves up on crowded streets, killing dozens. Israeli police have shot at demonstrating Palestinians, killing young men armed only with rocks. Tension is constant in the holy city.

In Jerusalem, Israel, the Dome of the Rock, one of Islam's holiest shrines, sits atop the Temple Mount. Below is the Western Wall of the Second Temple, also known as the Wailing Wall, a very holy site of Judaism.

On the other side of the Middle East, Saudi Arabia is home to the two holiest cities in Islam—Mecca and Medina. It was here that Muhammad preached, and from which his faith began to spread throughout the Middle East. These cities are sacred to every Muslim in the world. Five times a day, Muslims turn toward Mecca and pray. More than a million believers

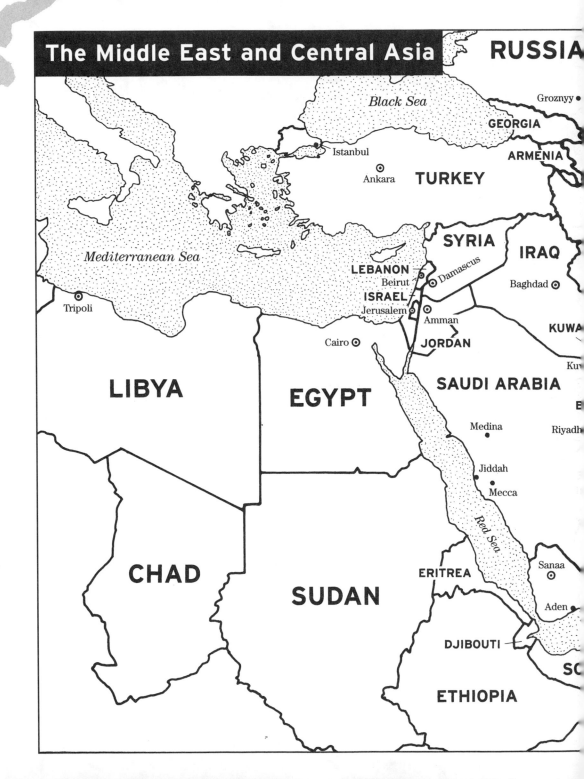

The Middle East and Central Asia

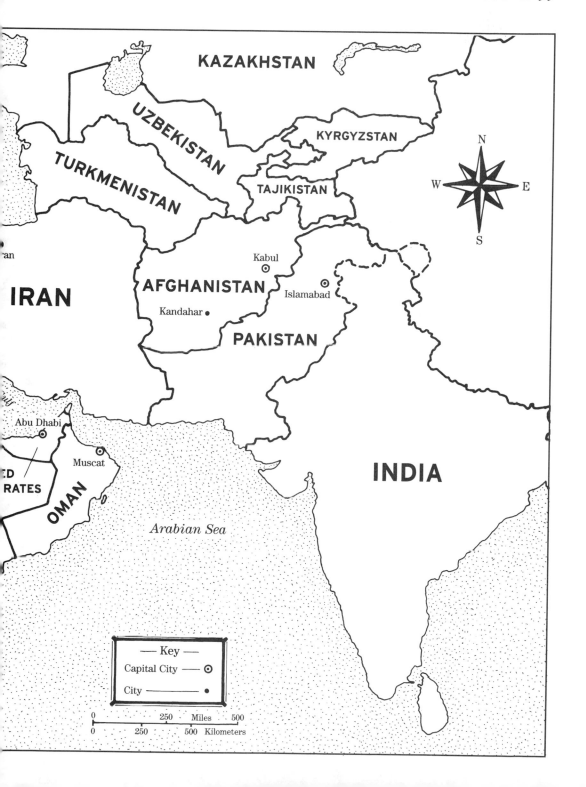

arrive in the city every year to make their sacred pilgrimage. What happens in Saudi Arabia is just as important to Muslims as what happens in Jerusalem is to Jews. The Saudi king is considered special, because he is responsible for protecting the two holiest cities.

Many Middle Eastern Muslims were angered when U.S. soldiers came to Saudi Arabia in preparation for the Gulf War in 1991. The dictator of Iraq, Saddam Hussein, and his armies had invaded neighboring Kuwait, a tiny country sandwiched between Iraq and Saudi Arabia. The rest of the world worried that Iraq would attack the Saudis next. The Saudi royal family allowed America and other nations to send troops to Arabia to defend them and to free Kuwait. To more conservative Muslims, it was sacrilegious to have these non-Muslim troops walking on the sacred ground of Arabia. Some of the soldiers were women who walked around without wearing veils. But the U.S. troops' presence also reminded Muslims around the world that the Saudis had felt they had no choice but to turn to non-Muslim nations to protect their holy land from Iraq. And U.S. troops have stayed in Arabia since the war, upsetting them further.

The Middle East matters because of economics.

WHY ARE there American soldiers in places like Saudi Arabia, Kuwait, Qatar, Bahrain, and Oman? After all, that part of the Middle East is largely desert. But the desert lies atop some of the largest oil deposits in the world. Towering rigs sit there, pumping out oil that can be used as fuel or as a crucial ingredient in thousands of products. It can also be refined into

5:00   6:00   7:00   8:00   9:00   ▼ 9:32 A.M.   10:00   11:00

9/11/01
A M   All financial markets in the United States are closed.

gasoline for cars. That oil has brought new wealth to the countries of the
Persian Gulf region in the Middle East.

American soldiers are stationed in the Persian Gulf to protect these
countries from attack by other countries like Iraq. America is so dependent
on this oil that to have it cut off would cripple our economy. During the Gulf
War, with Kuwait isolated from the rest of the world, oil and gas prices rose
dramatically in the United States. A more serious crisis took place in 1973,
when the Persian Gulf states decided to cut back on oil production so that
the price would go up. They did this partially to make more money, and partially to punish America for supporting Israel in the latest war between the
Arabs and the Jewish nation. The resulting gas shortage in America stalled

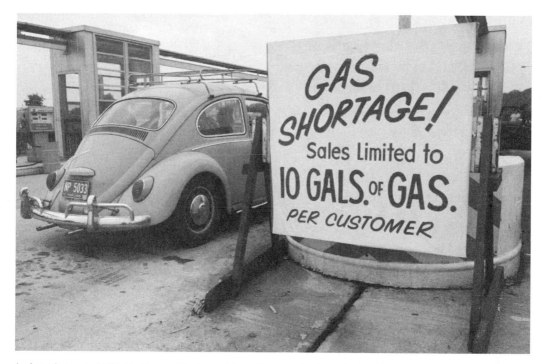

A sign at a gas station in Connecticut proclaims the gas shortage during the energy crisis of the 1970s.

OPEC

HOW DID the countries of the Persian Gulf effectively hold America hostage in 1973? OPEC cut back on oil production. Oil became scarcer and the price went up. OPEC, which stands for Organization of the Petroleum Exporting Countries, is an affiliation of eleven developing nations who rely heavily on oil production in their economies. To ensure stability, they meet at least twice a year and set production levels. Because OPEC nations produce 40 percent of the world's crude oil, they can effectively control prices around the world.

Not all OPEC members are in the Middle East. The current members include:

Algeria	Nigeria
Indonesia	Qatar
Iran	Saudi Arabia
Iraq	United Arab Emirates
Kuwait	Venezuela
Libya	

the entire economy. As fuel became scarce and expensive, factories could not afford to run full-time—they cut back their employees' work hours (and their paychecks). Trucks couldn't move products from one end of the country to the other. The power and heat in people's homes kept going out. Long lines formed at gas stations, and the government limited people to ten gallons of gas a week.

It's important to remember, though, that not every nation in the Middle East produces oil. Outside of the gulf region, there is little. Countries like Jordan and Egypt have been left out of the oil boom, and their economies have struggled. And the boom has not made life perfect in the gulf states either. The undemocratic governments of those countries control the economies tightly, and profits are kept by the rulers and a privileged few. Rulers like the Saudi king have used the money for huge modernization projects, but also wasted a lot of the money on extravagant palaces. Average citizens have never seen most of the money, and their lives have not improved very much. And because oil continues to be the only profitable industry in these nations, their economic growth has been limited. When oil prices drop, their entire economy shrivels.

The Middle East matters because it is politically unstable.

BECAUSE THE Middle East is so important in religion and economics, the rest of the world does not want to see it explode politically. Many of the countries in the Middle East are politically unstable. The governments don't always do such a good job running their countries. There is a lot of corruption and repression, and the people are trapped in poverty. Most of these rulers are either kings or dictators—they don't have to do what the people want, and they don't have to run for reelection. When a government keeps its people in misery for so long, there is the constant threat of rebellion from terrorists, mutinous army troops, or the general population.

If a revolution led to chaos in one or more countries, the world economy could be hurt by losing access to oil. And members of three major religions could be upset by the sight of the Holy Land in trouble. For these reasons, the U.S., as the world's only superpower, has kept a close eye on what goes on in the Middle East.

As long as much of the Middle East is ruled by corrupt or repressive governments, there is a danger the people will rebel. When the people continue to suffer, they look for someone to blame. Many blame their leaders and the countries which have been friendly to those leaders. And some blame the nations that have been successful while many Middle Eastern countries have gone from an empire to part of the third world.

6.
Why did the terrorists target the United States?

HEARING OSAMA bin Laden's hatred of America in his taped messages to the world, or the resentment of Muslims interviewed on the streets in the Middle East, many Americans in the weeks after September 11th asked themselves, Why do they hate us? To most Americans, the Middle East is a far-off place they rarely thought about before 9/11. But in the Middle East, Americans and the United States are resented and looked at with suspicion. There are several reasons for that.

Why do some people in the Middle East resent America?

TO MANY Middle Eastern people, America is an outside invader. Because of the Middle East's oil and its central location, our troops occupy bases scattered across the Persian Gulf region in the heart of the Middle East. As the most powerful nation on earth, America can go wherever it wants to but doesn't always think about what is best for the locals. Because we don't want Middle Eastern countries to collapse in a revolution and be taken over by rulers less friendly to us, our leaders have meddled in the nations' affairs, allowing dictators and kings to repress their people. We also support Israel, which many Muslims see as Muslim land under Jewish occupation.

But there is also a much deeper resentment, and it goes back centuries. America today is prosperous and successful, while the Middle East struggles with poverty and misery. But one thousand years ago, the Islamic empire that grew after Muhammad's death was the most powerful on earth. It stretched from Spain and North Africa to the frontiers of China and India. Its citizens studied in the best schools, writing great literature and making important discoveries about medicine, the stars, and the planets. Muslim merchants controlled much of the trade between Europe and Asia. And because their empire was united by its religion—Islam— Muslims felt their greatness was a sign that Islam was superior to all other faiths, that Allah had rewarded them. The Christian nations of Europe, meanwhile, were living in a dark age, a backward time when education was unavailable to most people, and countries were constantly at war.

Several times the Islamic empire collapsed, but a new one always took its place. The last Islamic empire declined during the last half of the millennium, however, and ended for good in 1919. By contrast, most of Europe has experienced an age of prosperity and world dominance during the last two centuries. Today America, a nation begun largely by Christians from Europe, is the most powerful nation on earth. Meanwhile, the heart of the old empires—the Middle East—is considered third-world, or underdeveloped. The vast majority of people there, despite the oil boom, are poor. They can work hard and still not have enough to feed their families. And a quality education is hard to come by. Many of the best students travel to America to attend our universities because there is nothing as good back home.

12:00   1:00   2:00   3:00   4:00   5:00   6:00

Everywhere Muslims look there are signs of America's dominance. Neon signs and TV ads sell American products. U.S. companies see the Middle East as a valuable market. Every bottle of Coca-Cola sold there is a reminder of America's economic superiority. These countries' people cannot escape it. In his taped messages, Osama bin Laden can be seen wearing a Timex digital watch—most likely because it's much better than

Egyptian men play dominoes beneath an ad for Coke. The presence of American products in the Middle East is a constant reminder for some Muslims of America's economic power.

Middle Eastern watches. His own family (which has disowned him) made a corporate deal with an American company to bring Snapple to Saudi Arabia.

And America doesn't just export iced tea—we export values, often values that are foreign to the Middle East. Muslims in the Middle East see ads for American products that tell them they are not successful unless they earn plenty of money. They see American ads, movies, and TV shows with women wearing skimpy clothing or being aggressive leaders at work. Our messages seem to tell them how to live their lives. In America, these things don't seem odd to us—they reflect our values. But according to

Islamic tradition, faith should be the primary influence on how Muslims live their lives. Success and wealth are far less important.

Watching America's strength and the Middle East's weakness, many Muslims want to know: What went wrong? If Islam is the true faith, how could the Middle East have fallen so far? Some Middle Eastern Muslims believe there is nothing they can do about America's dominance, and try to succeed within our system. But they often resent America deep down, because our nation is more economically successful. The United States has created an economic system their nations can't seem to prosper in.

Other Middle Eastern Muslims argue that the key to success is to turn away from America, that embracing Western values is exactly what weakened the Muslim nations in the first place, and that they need to return to strict Islamic values. And many of the Muslims who believe this also believe it is America's fault that they ever turned from Islam: that America's actions—our meddling, our trade, our relations with them—are a modern crusade designed to weaken and destroy Islam. The last sura of the Qur'an, one of the best known, tells Muslims to follow God and avoid the Great Satan. In the Qur'an, Satan is an evil force who tempts man to leave the true faith and God. To those who believe Western values are destroying Islam, America is the Great Satan.

Why would America meddle in Middle Eastern politics?

AMERICA HAS sent large amounts of financial and military aid to many Middle Eastern countries for more than fifty years in an effort to keep those nations stable and loyal to the U.S. But while this has helped the men who govern those nations, it has often created deep resentment among average Middle Eastern people. They see our actions as meddling in their own affairs and as keeping them from political freedom on their own terms. To them, America is a nation that believes in freedom for its own people while helping dictators deny it to other people, just for America's own selfish reasons.

The Middle East was not a concern to America until after World War II. Great Britain and France had colonized the Middle East after the Islamic empire collapsed but they withdrew from the region after the war. Then the Cold War began, and America and the Soviet Union were locked in a bitter struggle, each trying to gain more allies than the other. America believed democracy was the best hope for the world. The Russians believed communism was the ideal form of government.

To both America and the Soviets, the newly established countries of the Middle East were just waiting to be converted into model versions of their preferred form of government. So the Soviets and Americans began trying to influence these nations' rulers, offering economic aid or weapons for the Middle Eastern militaries. The Soviet leaders believed it was their duty to spread communism throughout the world. Already, the Soviet Union had installed Communist governments in all the countries of eastern Europe. The Americans felt that if they didn't keep the Soviets from gaining new allies, the entire rest of the world would be ruled by communism and America would be threatened.

To the new leaders of the Middle Eastern nations, this was a great opportunity. Many of them had been put in power by Great Britain and France, their former colonial rulers, which made the people they governed suspicious of them. The leaders knew American or Soviet money could help keep them in power. Some Middle Eastern leaders were sus-

5:00   6:00   7:00   8:00   9:00   10:00   11:00

▼ 9:48 A.M.

9/11/01
A.M.   The U.S. Capitol is evacuated; other federal buildings in D.C. close.

picious of America, because of its close ties to Great Britain and France. And some thought communism, with its authoritarian rule, was more suited to Islamic traditional government—the caliph had been an authoritarian ruler. They accepted Soviet aid and began experimenting

Negotiating Peace in the Middle East

AMERICA HAS been an important part of the Middle East peace process, helping Israel and its Arab neighbors and the Palestinians negotiate agreements. A 1979 peace treaty between Israel and Egypt was signed at Camp David, the presidential retreat in Maryland, with President Jimmy Carter. This was a crucial first step toward peace, because Egypt became the first Middle Eastern nation to recognize Israel.

America also helped negotiate the 1993 Oslo Accord, a landmark treaty between Israel and the Palestinian Authority, that allowed Palestinians some degree of control over parts of the West Bank and the Gaza Strip, the two Palestinian areas Israel occupied in 1967.

But in the months leading up to and following the September 11th attacks, a new round of violence in Israel threatened to undo the Oslo Accord. The U.S. did not work actively to get both sides back to peace talks. President George W. Bush put most of the blame for the violence on the Palestinians because they launched terrorist attacks in Israel. But he said little about Israel's harsh responses to the attacks, which included sending tanks and soldiers into Palestinian refugee camps, detaining thousands of Palestinians, and killing hundreds who fought back.

The Arab world asked why America wouldn't do more to stop the bloodshed, and the U.S. government replied that it was the Palestinians' responsibility to stop all attacks before talks could resume. To Muslims, it was another example of America taking the Israelis' side in every argument.

with communism. But others thought the future lay with America, and were frightened by the Soviets' atheism, their belief that there is no god. They preferred a mostly Christian nation to a godless one. They turned to the U.S. for help.

In return for the Middle Eastern nations' loyalty, both America and the Soviets were ready with aid. Some nations have even taken support from both countries—Egypt accepted Soviet support until the 1980s, and now receives American aid. And Iraq accepted help from both countries until the Gulf War in 1991. After the Soviet Union dissolved in 1991, even more Middle Eastern nations turned to the U.S. In return, the U.S. has been allowed to set up military bases in several nations including Oman, Bahrain, and Qatar.

But all that aid did not necessarily help the people of these young nations. Leaders who accepted American help did not necessarily adopt democracy in return. Sometimes they used the American aid to oppress their citizens and keep themselves in power. That didn't concern the American government—it was far more important to the U.S. that the Soviets not gain any new allies. The United States government was so focused on keeping the Soviets out of the Middle East that it often ignored the needs of ordinary Middle Eastern citizens.

When did Middle Eastern resentment first explode?

AS THESE dictators took American aid to keep themselves in power, the Middle Eastern people's resentment began to grow. In their eyes, Americans believed in freedom for themselves but helped dictators

5:00   6:00   7:00   8:00   9:00   10:00   11:00

▼ 9:50 A.M.

9/11/01
A M   The 110-story south tower of the World Trade Center collapses.

repress other people. One Muslim nation where that resentment exploded was Iran. For almost thirty years, America helped keep the Iranian monarch, the shah, in power, despite his repressive rule, just to gain his loyalty and keep Iran and its valuable oil away from Soviet influence. Shah Mohammed Reza Pahlavi's family had ruled Iran since 1921. After World War II though, he began to lose power to his more democratic prime minister. The shah eventually left Iran. In 1953, worried that the Iranian communist party was about to seize control of the country, America's CIA helped soldiers loyal to the shah launch a coup, or revolt, and return him to power. To the Iranian people, America looked like a nation of hypocrites, returning a monarch to power while ignoring the people's desire for more freedom.

After regaining control, the shah was eager to modernize his nation, which had been poor for several centuries, so he accepted American and Western aid. But while he tried to bring Western ideas to Iran's economy and society, he refused to bring democracy to his government. He was afraid he would lose power again. He did invite American businesses into the country, though. Those businesses sold U.S. products, advertising them with images of women who did not keep themselves covered as Iranian women did. Some Iranians felt that their country was abandoning Islam, and the people began to see America as a dangerous influence. In 1979, the people rose up and overthrew the shah. Radical Muslim clerics led by the Ayatollah Ruhollah Khomeini, who saw the rebellion as a chance to bring more Islamic rule to Iran, took power. They blamed America for keeping the shah in power for so long.

Iranian students in the capital, Tehran, were so angry over America's role in the previous coup and its aid to the shah that they stormed the U.S. embassy and took fifty-two Americans inside hostage. They held them captive for more than a year, accusing them of being CIA agents who were helping the shah repress the people. Meanwhile, demonstrators took to the streets almost every day for months, burning American flags and chanting "Death to America." Despite the hostages' eventual release, Iran and America have been bitter enemies ever since.

Didn't America fight to help Muslim people during the Gulf War?

AMERICA HAS come to the aid of Muslim people before, but too often its actions have appeared self-serving. During the Gulf War, the Americans pushed the Iraqis out of Kuwait from bases in Saudi Arabia. But U.S. forces did not remove Iraqi dictator Saddam Hussein from power, despite his hostility toward the rest of the world and his longtime repression of the Iraqi people. Instead, the United Nations (U.N.) imposed sanctions—special economic and trade restrictions that are meant to force a nation to change its ways—on Iraq. The U.N. hoped to force Hussein to stop threatening his country's neighbors. Hussein told the world that the sanctions were keeping food and medicine from Iraqi children and were killing hundreds of thousands of people. Many Muslims believe the sanctions—which are still in place in 2002—are killing innocent Iraqis. In reality, Hussein has been stealing the food and medicine the U.N. gives him and starving his own people.

In the first year after the Gulf War, America was secretly helping Iraqi rebel groups who were trying to oust Hussein. But the dictator found out and sent troops in helicopters to kill the rebels. When the rebels asked the U.S. to send in American jets to stop the helicopters, they were

5:00   6:00   7:00   8:00   9:00   10:00   11:00

▼9:55 A.M.

9/11/01
A M

President Bush leaves Florida and heads to Barksdale
Air Force Base outside Shreveport, Louisiana.

During the hostage crisis in 1979, protestors angrily surrounded the U.S. embassy. Here, one protestor holds a poster of the Ayatollah Khomeini (left), while another has made a cardboard cutout of U.S. president Jimmy Carter being hanged on a scaffold.

ignored. The U.S. government under President George H. W. Bush—the same president who had liberated Kuwait—was afraid of involving U.S. troops in a dangerous mission. Without U.S. help, the rebels were defeated, and most were killed. When people throughout the Middle East saw the Americans abandon the rebels, it confirmed their suspicions that America was willing to fight to liberate Kuwait, an oil-rich monarchy and ally, but not to help the Iraqi people, who had little to offer America.

How does the Middle East feel about America's support for Israel?

AMERICA'S SUPPORT for Israel has created more Arab resentment of the U.S. than perhaps any other issue. To the Muslims of the Middle East, the creation of a Jewish state was nothing more than a hostile occupation of Muslim lands by European Jews. America's support has helped the Jews to keep those lands. When Great Britain decided to withdraw from Palestine in 1947, the United Nations voted to establish two nations there—a Palestinian state and a Jewish state. The Jews would get Israel because of the horrors of the holocaust, when more than six million European Jews were killed. But Arabs and Palestinians refused to accept the U.N.'s actions—they believed all Palestine should belong to Palestinians—and five Middle Eastern nations invaded in 1948. The Israelis fought back and defeated the Arabs in 1949 taking control of all of Palestine except the West Bank and Gaza Strip, which Jordan and Egypt took control of. With no state of their own, close to one million Palestinians moved to refugee camps in nearby Arab nations. In 1967, fearing attack by Egypt and Syria, Israel invaded and in six days took over the West Bank and Gaza Strip, where millions of Palestinians still lived. Israel has held the land ever since.

America did not originally support Israel in 1948. While many Americans sympathized with the plight of Jews during the holocaust, the U.S. government knew that helping Israel would upset the Arabs. But when the Soviets supported the Arab invasion of Israel, America put its resources behind the Israelis. The U.S. has continued to back Israel to this day. In 2002, the U.S. gave three billion dollars in aid to Israel, most of it military aid. The Israelis use American-built F-16 fighter jets and Apache

5:00   6:00   7:00   8:00   9:00   10:00   ▼ 9:58 A.M.   11:00

9/11/01
A.M.   An emergency dispatcher in Pennsylvania receives a call from a passenger on United Airlines Flight 93 who says, "We are being hijacked, we are being hijacked!"

helicopters to fight the Palestinians. The Arabs see this as America handing weapons to their enemy—proof that America hates Muslims.

While America has helped in the peace process between Israel and the Palestinians, it has traditionally sided with the Israelis, supporting the Jews' desire for security while mostly ignoring Palestinians' pleas for a homeland of their own. Meanwhile, many Arab leaders routinely speak of the Palestinians' suffering, and how Israel cruelly occupies their land with American help. It is not uncommon to see Middle Eastern people take to their streets, chanting repeatedly, "Death to Israel—and death to America."

Do some Muslims hate America just because it's America?

EVEN IF America withdrew its soldiers and its products from the Middle East tomorrow, a small group of Muslims would still feel the U.S. must be destroyed simply because it is the leading Western nation. That's because these radical Muslims believe Islam is at war with all nonbelievers. They follow a belief dating back to the seventh century that says the world consists of two houses—the House of Islam and the House of War, Dar al Islam and Dar al Harb. The House of War is the part of the world that has not embraced Allah. Today most Muslims obey Muhammad's call to respect other monotheistic religions. But a small minority, including Osama bin Laden and al Qaeda, think it is their holy duty to wage jihad against Dar al Harb. To them, there is no better way to show Islam's superiority than to take over and destroy the mightiest infidel nation of all—America. To them, the United States cannot do anything to change the fact that it is the Great Satan, and all Americans are legitimate targets.

7.
Why did we go
after Afghanistan?

THE REACTION to the deadly attacks on 9/11 was swift. Within a month, U.S. warplanes were launching missiles at Afghanistan, targeting the country's Taliban leadership and Osama bin Laden's al Qaeda network. To understand why America attacked Afghanistan, you have to know something of that country's tortured history.

America began its war on terror in Afghanistan because the Taliban, militant Islamists who had ruled the war-torn country for five years, were allowing bin Laden and his terrorists to use the country as their home base. Al Qaeda operated training camps in the deserts and caves of the countryside, teaching Muslims from around the world how to wage a holy war against the West. Several of the hijackers were trained there.

Why were these terrorists from all over able to use Afghanistan as their base? The answer lies in the nation's twenty-three-year war beginning in 1979. Al Qaeda was born in Afghanistan during a war that changed the face of Islam and created an entire generation of holy warriors. And the United States helped create it.

Where is Afghanistan?

MOHAMMED IQBAL, a famous Indian poet, once called Afghanistan the heart of Asia. The country, which is roughly the size of Texas, is not part of the Middle East. It lies in between the Middle East and the Far East—India, China, and the nations beyond. Sandwiched between Iran and Pakistan, with the former Soviet republics of central Asia to its north, Afghanistan's location has made it an important crossroads. The explorer and merchant Marco Polo crossed the nation while traveling to China in the late thirteenth century, one of many Europeans trying to make his fortune on the Silk Road, the main trading route between Europe and Asia. Today, truck driving smugglers travel the same roads to carry contraband—opium, counterfeit products, guns—between India and central Asia and even Russia. Several corporations have explored the idea of running lucrative oil and gas pipelines through Afghanistan, carrying fuel between central Asian oil fields and shipping ports on the Indian Ocean.

Afghanistan's location has also made it an appealing target for invaders, because it allowed them to reach valuable lands on the other side. The Macedonian king Alexander the Great conquered the nation in 330 B.C. Genghis Khan, ruler of the Mongolians, invaded in A.D. 1220. The land is not rich, despite its strategic value. Afghanistan is mostly desert and mountains. Only ten percent of the land can be farmed. For centuries, most people herded goats or sheep to make a living. The tall Hindu Kush mountains, which rise in parts to almost 25,000 feet, divide the country diagonally, cutting from the southwest to the northeast.

12:00   1:00   2:00   3:00   4:00   5:00   6:00

A small farming community in the Bayan valley sits at the foot of the Hindu Kush mountains.

The mountain peaks also divide the nation's various ethnic groups, who are predominantly Muslims, though not Arabs. In the valleys between the mountains live Persian-speaking Tajiks and the Hazarats, who are related to Mongolians. North of the mountains, on the flat steppes, are Turkic peoples, the Uzbeks and Turkmen. South of the mountains, dry plains and harsh deserts stretch from Iran to Pakistan. Here the Pashtuns live.

Afghanistan's harsh landscape has kept most of these ethnic groups separate. Even today, it can be hard for people to travel from one area to another, so interaction is rare. This has left many of the people fiercely independent and has made Afghanistan hard to rule. Even though most of the population converted to Islam in the late seventh century, their common faith has not united them. The people identify much more with members of their own ethnicities and tribes than with fellow Muslims. And while the rulers of the Islamic empire in the Middle East took their authority from God, Afghan kings ruled by the authority of the Loya

5:00   6:00   7:00   8:00   9:00   10:00   11:00

▼ 10:00 A.M.

9/11/01
A M

United Airlines Flight 93 crashes in a field in Shanksville, Pennsylvania, 80 miles southeast of Pittsburgh.

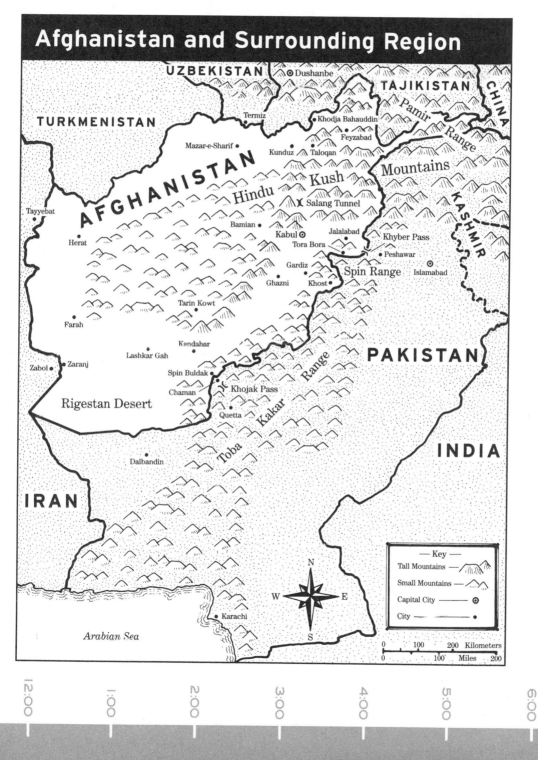

Afghanistan and Surrounding Region

Jirga, a council of tribal leaders. Despite their diversity, the one thing Afghans have never tolerated is foreigners coming into their country and telling them what to do.

Why did the Soviet Union invade Afghanistan?

EVEN BEFORE Russian soldiers invaded Afghanistan in December 1979, the Soviet Union had played a large role in recent Afghan history. Long a poor country, Afghanistan's government began taking financial and military aid from the Soviets in 1956. The communist Soviets were eager to control Afghanistan—it would put them closer to Iran and the oil-rich Persian Gulf in the West and Pakistan and India in the East.

To gain that control, the Soviets encouraged communist officers of the Afghan army to overthrow the king. After they did, a communist government was established in 1978. But most Afghans did not want a communist government, because communists advocate atheism—not believing in God or religion—and because they resented foreigners' having such influence. When the Afghan people began resisting the new government, the Soviets sent in their army to calm things down. They figured their troops would restore order, put the Afghan communists firmly in charge, and leave within a year.

But in a matter of months, the Soviet army was being harassed by constant guerilla attacks by ordinary Afghans who were furious over this foreign invasion. After watching the Ayatollah Khomeini create an Islamic republic in Iran, the Soviets were worried the same thing could happen in Afghanistan. They were even more determined to control the tiny nation.

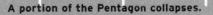

A portion of the Pentagon collapses.

They fought back against the guerillas. But while the Soviets quickly took control of the cities, the rebels remained in control of the countryside. These rebels called themselves *mujaheddin*, the name given to holy warriors who fight in a jihad for Islam. The Soviets tried everything to crush them. But they couldn't. The small bands of mujaheddin were too hard to pin down, the Afghan landscape was too harsh and the weather too cold, and few of the Afghan people would help the Soviets. After ten years, the Soviets withdrew and left the Afghan communists to fend for themselves.

How did the U.S. get involved?

THE MUJAHEDDIN fought bravely but they had help. The United States did not want Afghanistan to become another Russian province, especially with the oil-rich Middle East nearby, so the U.S. government gave money and weapons to the Afghan fighters to help them fight the Soviets. During the decade long conflict, America gave more than four billion dollars to the mujaheddin. And we weren't the only ones. Many other nations saw the Afghans' battle as a noble attempt to fight off a much more powerful aggressor. European nations chipped in. And Saudi Arabia matched U.S. donations dollar for dollar. The Saudis saw this as a fight by Islam against an infidel invader.

For the U.S., getting the money and weapons to the mujaheddin was something to be done in secret. The U.S. was loudly denouncing the Soviet intervention. To avoid looking hypocritical, the U.S. claimed it was staying out of the Afghan conflict. So it used its ally Pakistan as a go-between to hide what it was doing. The CIA and the Saudi government transferred money to bank accounts controlled by the Inter-Services Intelligence (ISI),

Pakistan's intelligence agency. The ISI then funneled the money to some of the mujaheddin leaders. The CIA also bought weapons from other countries and secretly shipped them to Pakistan where the ISI distributed them.

By letting the ISI choose which mujaheddin got U.S. help, the CIA was letting Pakistan decide which of the mujaheddin groups had the most success. The ISI channeled most of the foreign money to the more Islamist mujaheddin groups which were emphasizing the idea of the fight as a holy war between Muslims and atheist infidels (instead of mainly a battle against foreign invaders).

Why was Pakistan involved in the Afghan war?

PAKISTAN AND Afghanistan share more than a common border—they have a common history. Most people in both countries are Muslim, and a large chunk of both nations' populations belong to the Pashtun tribe. So what happened in the Afghan fight against the Soviets was of great importance to Pakistanis. And for domestic political reasons, Pakistan's government was eager to make the fight in Afghanistan a holy war. This government, which had come to power in a military coup in 1979, was trying to gain the support of large Islamist political parties at home to help cement its rule. By supporting the more Islamist Afghan mujaheddin, the government won the support of Pakistani Islamists. Many of these Islamists went to Afghanistan to help fight the Soviets. Pakistan already had a fiercely Islamic identity. The nation had been carved out of India in 1947 when the British granted India independence. The Hindus and Muslims in the colony had clashed so much that Pakistan was created to give Muslims their own country. Since then, Pakistan and India had fought several wars over Kashmir, a province both countries claimed. With U.S. money, Pakistan was now encouraging an Islamic identity as strong as their own in Afghanistan.

Who were the Mujaheddin?

WHILE THE mujaheddin called themselves "holy warriors," they mostly saw themselves as ordinary Afghans defending their homes. It helped their cause that they were fighting for their Islamic faith as well, but for many it was not their main motivation. When they decided to fight the Soviets, they fell back on their traditional tribal loyalties. Local leaders would assemble small bands of fighters and start launching guerilla attacks on Soviet troops in their territory. The Afghans could never defeat the Russians in a traditional battle, because of the Russian's superior numbers and weapons, so they mounted constant small attacks until the Russians decided the war wasn't worth their blood and sweat. Mujaheddin would hide and wait for a Russian convoy, launch a quick attack, and then flee before the Russians could counterattack. They would steal Russian supplies. They would make it hard for the Russians to move around. All of this was to prove to the Soviets that Afghanistan was impossible to control.

As the war dragged on, though, the mujaheddin's struggle became popular in other Islamic nations. Muslims everywhere, but especially in the Middle East, which had been pushed around by more powerful countries for the last sixty years, saw the war as a jihad. Mullahs began calling for Muslims to donate to charities to help the Afghans. And beginning around 1984, young Muslim men, especially Arabs, began traveling to Pakistan to take up arms and fight in Afghanistan. Many Pakistanis also crossed the border to fight. Two years later, thousands of foreign Muslim fighters were there. The United States' involvement in the war had made victory seem possible. Many of these jihadis, as they called themselves, had been sent by their mosques or by religious schools called *madrassahs*, their tickets paid for by Muslim charities. Saudi Arabian Airlines began offering large discounts on flights to Pakistan.

Most of these young men were idealists and eager to fight. Some were Islamist militants whose own governments were happy to see them leave. Once in Afghanistan, however, these men realized there were thousands of Muslims just like them who wanted to fight for their faith. They called themselves the "Arab Afghans." They began to share their knowledge and ideas. And they also began looking for more support. One of their leaders was Osama bin Laden. He was then just a wealthy Saudi, only twenty-eight years old. But he traveled throughout the Middle East, appealing for financial help. The money and weapons and new jihadis kept coming.

What happened after the Soviets withdrew?

IT WAS only after the Soviets gave up and abandoned Afghanistan that the U.S. government began to realize what a dangerous force it had helped unleash. Thousands of young, militant Muslims had come together to fight, and had learned that they could defeat a superpower in the name of Islam. In 1989, the U.S. asked Pakistan to begin arresting the Arab Afghans and deport them back to their home countries. The ISI deported the Arabs, and urged the Pakistani mujaheddin to refocus their attentions on Kashmir. They began attacking Indian soldiers and civilians in Kashmir, hoping to wrest the disputed province from India. The Arab Afghans returned to their home countries, and their governments were

5:00 6:00 7:00 8:00 9:00 10:00 10:22 A.M. ▼ 11:00

9/11/01 A.M. The State and Justice Departments in Washington are evacuated.

not thrilled to see them back. The militants who returned home began working to overthrow their own governments, which they felt were disloyal to Islam. Some would be exiled, many finding sanctuary in Europe.

As for the Afghans themselves, it would take almost three more years for the mujaheddin to defeat the Afghan communist government that the Russians had abandoned. In 1992, they conquered Kabul, the capital city. But the mujaheddin leaders almost immediately began fighting each other. One prominent leader, Gulbuddin Hikmatyar, unhappy with his position in the new government, left Kabul and ordered his troops to shell the city. In the countryside, local warlords ruled small chunks of the country through sheer force. The war never really stopped—the mujaheddin just switched from fighting the Soviets to fighting among themselves. Travelers faced the risk of robbery by marauding gangs. Traders driving

Facts about Afghanistan

SIZE: 250,000 square miles (a little smaller than Texas) **POPULATION:** 26,813,057 (2001 estimate) **LIFE EXPECTANCY:** 46 years **ETHNIC GROUPS:** Pashtun 38%, Tajik 25%, Hazarat 19%, Uzbek 6%, minor ethnic groups (Aimak, Turkmen, Baloch, and others) 12% **LANGUAGES:** Dari (similar to Persian) 50%, Pashtu 35%, Turkic languages (primarily Uzbek and Turkmen) 11%, thirty minor languages (primarily Balochi and Pashai) 4% **INDUSTRIES:** World's largest grower of opium poppies (from which heroin is made), smuggling, herding goats and sheep, oil and gas, mining **LITERACY:** (1999 estimate) men 47%, women 15%

on the highways were stopped by soldiers asking them to pay tolls that were really bribes. For the average Afghan, life wasn't getting any better even with the Soviets gone.

What has life been like for the Afghan people?

AMERICA'S WAR began on September 11th. But the Afghans' war began twenty-three years earlier when the Soviets invaded. More than two million Afghans died in the fighting. An entire generation of children have grown into adults knowing nothing but war. Many have never known a home. More than three million refugees fled to Pakistan and Iran to get away from the fighting, living in temporary camps that have become permanent towns, eating the scarce food donated by relief agencies.

To a child growing up, Afghanistan has been a cruel place. Many children have died from malnourishment. Long droughts have made food scarce. Schools have been few and far between. Running and playing hasn't been safe either. The Soviets littered the countryside with millions of land mines designed to kill the mujaheddin. Many killed or maimed kids instead. Childhood has been short, too. Some children became soldiers at only thirteen or fourteen years old.

Many Afghans felt abandoned by the United States and the rest of the world. America forgot about the distant country the moment the Soviets withdrew. It was 1989, and the Soviet empire was showing signs of collapse. Eastern Europe was beginning to move toward democracy after almost fifty years of communism. Afghanistan was not a priority for the U.S. anymore. But for the Afghan people, the war was still going on, the

5:00 6:00 7:00 8:00 9:00 10:00 10:24 A.M. ▼ 11:00

The FAA reports that all transatlantic aircraft flying into the U.S. are being diverted to Canada.

Afghan children play on a burned Soviet army tank in the village of Malaspa, Panjshir Valley.

country was in ruins, and everyone had a gun, many of which had been sent by the United States.

For the Arabs and Afghans, the West's abandonment was a sign of American cruelty. Afghanistan became "one of the world's orphaned conflicts—the ones that the West, selective and promiscuous in its inattention, happens to ignore," said the Egyptian Boutros Boutros-Ghali in 1995, when he was Secretary General of the United Nations. One Arab Afghan put it another way: "The Russians lost. The Muslims died. The Americans won."

But the Americans did not win. While the U.S. helped defeat the Soviets, it helped to create the Arab Afghans and al Qaeda. And by abandoning Afghanistan to civil war and misery, America made it easy for the Taliban to come to power.

8.
Who are the Taliban?

THE TALIBAN were strict Islamist Afghans who formed a government made up of old mujaheddin from the Soviet war and young religious students. They ruled Afghanistan for six years, leading the country into further misery and allowing al Qaeda to operate training camps for thousands of terrorists. Osama bin Laden couldn't have built al Qaeda without the Taliban, who allowed him to operate freely in Afghanistan.

With the Soviet Union's withdrawal in 1989 and the American abandonment, Afghanistan had descended into an utter chaos of constant war, crime, and starvation. The leading mujaheddin factions had formed a government, led by a president and council of former fighters, that ruled in Kabul; but they were so busy fighting each other that they had no control over the rest of the country. Instead, other mujaheddin fighters had become local warlords, ruling by force with the help of gangs of former soldiers.

The only profitable way to make a living for the average Afghan was by growing opium poppies, which are used to make heroin. Many farmers turned to the drug crop, while other Afghans eked out a meager living herding sheep and goats. But hundreds of thousands of Afghans fled to

Pakistan and Iran, joining the millions who had lived in permanent refugee camps since the Soviet war. In this atmosphere of chaos, the Taliban emerged.

Where did the Taliban come from?

THE TALIBAN movement was started and led by Mohammed Omar, a mullah, or Islamic teacher, from Singesar, a small village in southern Afghanistan near the city of Kandahar. Little is known about Omar. Even while ruling Afghanistan, he almost always refused to meet with foreigners, and he has only been caught on film a few times. He fought with the mujaheddin against the Soviets, losing his right eye during a battle. He then taught Islam at a small madrassah, or religious school, where young boys studied the Qur'an. But in 1994, he and a band of men slowly took control of Kandahar Province. They called themselves Taliban, or students of Islam.

No one is quite sure how the Taliban movement began. The most popular story, though Afghans are not sure it's true, is that Omar launched a daring raid with some of his friends in 1994. The southern Afghan city of Kandahar was one of the country's most dangerous at the time, divided up by warlords who were always fighting each other for control. One day, a local warlord kidnapped several young girls and boys, shaved their heads and allowed his soldiers to abuse them. Outraged, Mullah Omar gathered some thirty armed men and went to the warlord's headquarters. They attacked and killed the soldiers, then hung the warlord's body from the barrel of his tank to show that immoral people like him would be punished.

As Omar and his followers continued fighting warlords who were abusing their power, they began to recruit young men to their cause.

While the top two dozen Taliban leaders were former mujaheddin, the majority of their followers were too young to have fought the Soviets. They were members of the refugee generation that grew up in camps in Pakistan's Northwest Frontier Province. They respected the Taliban's strict, conservative Islamic principles, and flocked into Afghanistan and toward Kandahar, providing Omar and his men with a growing army.

What was the Taliban interpretation of Islam?

AS WE'VE seen in previous chapters, throughout history people have used religion to justify violence and intolerance. All major religions have been used this way, but the Taliban's radical interpretation of Islam was an especially severe corruption of religion. And their beliefs reflected their own violent nature more than any true meaning of the religion of Muhammad.

Since Islam first reached them in the seventh century, the people of Afghanistan have actually had one of the more tolerant interpretations of the faith. While the religion was an important part of most Afghans' lives (even communist government officials—supposedly atheist—used to pray in their offices), Afghans did not believe in judging each other's spirituality. Islam was not a major part of the government either. But the Taliban, who believed that a more radical, strict version of Islam was the only way to save the country from destruction, brought a new, harsh tone to Afghan religious life.

The Taliban's Islam had its roots in Pakistan. It evolved from Deobandi Islam, a branch of the religion developed in the 1800s in India and Pakistan, whose creators originally meant to adapt Islam to modern times and life under British colonial rule. But it changed in the 1980s while the Soviet-Afghan war raged. An Islamist political party called Jamiat e Ulema Islam adapted the Deobandi teachings to its own militant beliefs about the evil of non-Muslims such as the Soviets.

To spread its teachings, Jamiat opened hundreds of new madrassahs in the poorer sections of Pakistan, mostly in southern Baluchistan and the Northwest Frontier Province, where Pakistani members of the Pashtun tribe and all the Afghan refugees, most of whom also were Pashtun, lived. Pakistan's public schools were closing because of a lack of money, so for many poor families the madrassahs were the only affordable schools. In 1971 there were 900 madrassahs. By 1988 there were 8,000 receiving public funds and another 25,000 small unregistered ones. Inside the madrassahs, thousands of poor young Pakistani and Afghan boys learned the Qur'an and the mullahs' strict beliefs, many of which had more to do with Pashtun tribal tradition than anything Muhammad had said.

The Pashtun tribe has been one of South Asia's fiercest for centuries. The Pashtuns' territory comprises eastern Afghanistan and northwest Pakistan. They have always fought other groups' attempts to control them, so much so that even today Pakistan's government exercises little control over Pashtuns living in Pakistan. Those Pashtuns have their own courts and rarely answer to the Pakistani police or army. All Pashtuns live by a strict tribal code—Pashtunwali—with tough penalties for crime and strong rules for how women should behave.

Not all Pashtuns joined the Taliban, in fact the majority did not. But most of the young men who did had grown up in these strict madrassahs. The Islam they learned is simple, uncompromising, and backward. They were taught that modern society is evil, that entertainment and culture—

movies, television, music, and art—have nothing to do with faith and are evil, and that women must be separated from men at all times to prevent temptation. They also were taught that the West is a land of infidels and must be ignored or, if possible, destroyed. As the students grew older, their teachers ordered them to go to Afghanistan, telling them Mullah Omar's quest to take over the country was a holy jihad. And when Omar needed reinforcements, the mullahs would close their schools and send thousands of younger students—fifteen and sixteen year olds—across the border to fight.

Traditional Islam has always been a religion of great scholarly works and debate, but the Taliban beliefs were set in stone and there was no room for debate. Any Afghan who disagreed with them was considered an infidel who deserved punishment or death. Because most Afghans were not raised under this harsh form of Islam, as the Taliban took over the country they made life very difficult for the people.

How did the Taliban take over Afghanistan?

IN 1994, the Taliban were still just a ragtag band of fighters in Kandahar. But as their numbers grew, they began to take over more of the poor city and surrounding provinces. The Taliban needed more than just student fighters, however—they needed money and guns. They turned to Pakistan.

The Taliban efforts to bring law and order to Kandahar province had attracted Pakistan's attention. With a hostile India on one border, Pakistan was looking for a friend in Afghanistan. Because of its own large Pashtun population, Pakistan saw the Taliban, most of whom were

5:00   6:00   7:00   8:00   9:00   10:00   11:00

10:30 A.M. ▼

9/11/01   New York State governor George Pataki declares a state of emergency.

Pashtun, as a potential ally. Its government gave money and guns to Mullah Omar's men. Pakistan told its border guards to allow all the young students from the madrassahs to cross into Afghanistan to join Omar.

The Taliban also found another source of money. Afghanistan is a crucial route for truckers smuggling all sorts of goods—drugs, counterfeit goods, fuel. With the warlords in charge, even the smugglers were being robbed in Afghanistan. Dozens of armed gangs would lay giant chains across the highways, blocking the trucks' passage unless the smugglers paid

A rare portrait of Taliban leader Mullah Mohammed Omar appeared on the front page of the Algerian daily newspaper *El Youm*, October 2001.

huge bribes. The smugglers promised Mullah Omar a monthly payment if the Taliban could keep the roads open. With their new backers, the Taliban had enough money to conquer Kandahar by defeating some warlords in battle and bribing others to surrender. From there, they spread out into the rest of the country.

In the next two years the Taliban took control of southern Afghanistan. But their biggest challenge came in 1996, as they prepared to attack Kabul, the Afghan capital. If they could capture Kabul, they could legitimately call themselves the rulers of Afghanistan and would control more than half the country. To inspire his men for the fight, Mullah Omar gave himself a new rank—*Amir ul Momineen*, a sacred title meaning "Commander of the Faithful." By giving himself such a holy title, he was hoping to prove to his men that this was a sacred jihad they were fighting. He then went one step further. He went into Kandahar's holiest mosque and brought out a cloak that legend said belonged to Muhammad himself. The cloak has long been Afghanistan's most sacred relic. Omar showed the cloak to his followers and then put it on. To many Muslims such an act would be sacrilegious, but by this time the Taliban believed Omar was holier than any man except Muhammad. His act convinced them they were fighting a holy jihad.

In Kabul, the most legendary mujaheddin from the Soviet war, Ahmed Shah Massoud, led an army of soldiers trying to keep the Taliban out of the city for as long as possible. But the mujaheddin leaders were still fighting each other, and the Taliban were able to bribe many of the commanders to abandon Massoud shortly before a new attack. The city fell in September 1996, and Massoud and his army were forced to flee north.

While the Taliban had conquered the capital and half the country, their war was about to get more difficult. In the chaos following the Soviet war, the various Afghan ethnic groups had become much more suspicious of each other. Almost entirely Pashtun, the Taliban weren't welcome in the northern half of the country, which was dominated by other ethnic groups. Also, the people living under Taliban rule in the south quickly grew tired of the harsh Islamic government being forced on them by their new rulers. The majority of the population did not share the Taliban's religious fervor. Kabul, a cosmopolitan city with universities, especially chafed under the Taliban. And Mullah Omar and his inner circle were wary and suspicious of non-Taliban Afghans trying to advise or participate in their government.

As the Taliban moved north and began to fight Tajiks, Uzbeks, and Hazaras, they seemed to be acting on ethnic hatred rather than religious fervor. They treated non-Pashtuns incredibly harshly, committing repeated atrocities. For example, in 1997, after suffering several losses, the Taliban surrounded the Hazarat city of Bamian, starving the Shi'ite population until it surrendered. A few months later they took the ancient northern city of Mazar-e-Sharif. For six days, they massacred the population and left the corpses to rot in the streets.

Despite their progress in the north, the Taliban campaign stalled in 1998. Massoud had united the remaining opposition forces as the Northern Alliance. The Taliban had more men and controlled ninety percent of the country, but Massoud was the smarter strategist and was receiving money and weapons from countries who opposed the Taliban, including Iran and even his old enemy Russia. The fight bogged down in a constant, bloody war for the next three years.

What was life like under the Taliban?

IMAGINE IF every woman disappeared from view. Imagine if all the girls in your school were forced to stay at home and any teachers who weren't men were sent home too. Imagine if your dad could be beaten if he didn't grow a beard. Imagine if your mom could not talk to any man except her husband and relatives. Imagine if you went to see a soccer game and instead were forced to watch an execution.

The Taliban had come of age in violence, war, and misery, and that's what they brought to the Afghan people. The government issued constant laws to ban any celebration or fun that could distract people from Islam. The laws seemed to come more from a desire to force the people into submission than from any deeper religious meaning. The center of this religious oppression was the Department for the Protection of Virtue and Prevention of Vice. Armed young Taliban from the department patrolled the streets of Kabul, Kandahar, and other cities, enforcing the department's strict rules. They beat any man or woman who did not obey, with a whip or club. A boy flying a kite could be beaten. A women whose ankles were seen could be beaten. A man who didn't rush to the mosque at prayer time could be beaten.

In the spring of 1997, the Taliban lifted the ban on soccer games. They asked international aid groups to help them rebuild the Kandahar soccer stadium. Eager to help the people, the groups happily agreed. When games began in the new stadium, the groups were horrified to discover that the Taliban had allowed the games so more people would be present for executions. During halftime, prisoners were marched out for various offenses—theft, adultery, murder. Their hands were cut off, they were shot in the head, or sometimes hung from goal posts. The Taliban made sure the people watched.

Because the Taliban grew up either in all-male madrassahs or on the battlefield with only fellow male soldiers, they had no understanding of women. They thought women were dangerous, weak, and not to be trusted. So it is no surprise that no group faced more hardship under the Taliban than women. All women were forbidden to work. Because more than 70 percent of teachers in Afghanistan were women, most schools shut down. Girls were forbidden to attend school anyway. The Taliban realized they

5:00   6:00   7:00   8:00   9:00   10:00   11:00 A.M.

9/11/01
A.M.   Mayor Giuliani orders lower Manhattan evacuated.

needed female nurses to treat women in hospitals. So the only women allowed to work were nurses and doctors. Health care for women suffered. If no female doctors could be found to treat a woman, a male doctor had to don a veil and relay instructions to a female nurse who actually touched the patient. Many women died of disease and in childbirth.

Afghanistan's wars had raged for so long that many women's husbands had died in battle. Suddenly, these women weren't allowed to work, so they had no income. They were forced to beg to support their children. Because the enforcers of the Department for the Protection of Virtue often harassed women who were out in public without their husbands, most women tried to avoid leaving their homes at all. If they did, they had

Underground schools for girls

AFGHAN WOMEN and girls lived a horrible life under the Taliban, but many found secret ways to resist the regime's strict edicts. Banned from their old schools, some Afghan girls began to attend secret, underground classes. Female teachers who were forbidden to work would teach small groups of girls in private apartments. They took a big risk. If the Taliban caught them, both teachers and students would be severely punished. The Taliban could even execute the teachers. The girls often kept copies of the Qur'an nearby in case they were discovered—it was the only book they were allowed to be studying. Or they would study in the kitchen and keep pots on the stove, pretending they were having a cooking class.

After the Taliban lost power, girls rushed back to the schools. Hundreds signed up for classes at Kabul University. But an entire generation of young women are now years behind in their studies. With no hope of an education or a job, some girls had gotten married as young as fourteen and begun having children. Now many are trying to catch up, and many of the underground schools have been converted into study sessions to help them.

An Afghan refugee girl sits among a group of women in burqas at a refugee camp in Pakistan. The Taliban forced Afghan women to wear burqas whenever they were in public.

to wear a burqa, a traditional Afghan garment that covers the entire body including hands and feet, and has only a tiny mesh screen to see out of. It made women almost invisible on the streets, easy to ignore. The vanishing of an entire gender had enormous effects. Half of the country's workforce was sidelined, hurting the economy.

The Taliban took the joy out of the Afghan people's lives. Kite flying was forbidden. Television was forbidden. Dancing was forbidden. Music was forbidden. Long hair on men was forbidden, yet beards had to be long. Gambling and cards were forbidden. The country began to slip into a dark age.

Why did the Taliban allow Osama bin Laden to live in Afghanistan?

NOT LONG after the Taliban captured Kabul, Mullah Omar struck up a friendship with Osama bin Laden, a former Arab-Afghan leader who had been exiled from both his native Saudi Arabia and Sudan and was living near Kabul. Omar invited him and his family to Kandahar. Bin Laden quickly became an important ally. He gave one of his daughters to Omar in marriage, and he used his fortune to aid the Taliban. He and Omar shared a hatred of the West because it abandoned Afghanistan after the Soviet war. Both believed the Muslim world needed a new, Islamist ruler. Bin Laden hoped all of the Muslim world would soon be ruled by a strict amir, or leader, like Omar. The Taliban saw bin Laden as a way to spread their revolution. He founded training camps for terrorists from all over the world. In return for the Taliban's support, many of those al Qaeda fighters fought for the Taliban against the Northern Alliance.

Why did the Taliban fall so quickly?

ON SEPTEMBER 9th, 2001, Osama bin Laden gave a gift to the Taliban: He helped them get rid of the Northern Alliance commander they had been unable to defeat. Two Arab assassins now believed to be members of al Qaeda sat down for an interview with Alliance leader Ahmed Shah Massoud. They had told him they were journalists. One set off a bomb in a camera and Massoud was mortally wounded—he died a few days later.

12:00   1:00   2:00   3:00   4:00   5:00   6:00

▼ 11:45 A.M.

The president arrives at Barksdale Air Force Base in Louisiana.

9/11/01

The Taliban believed the entire country would soon be under their control. By killing Massoud before al Qaeda attacked New York and Washington, bin Laden may have been trying to destroy the Northern Alliance so that if America came to Afghanistan to fight the Taliban and al Qaeda, it would not find an eager ally.

In October 2001, when U.S. planes began to bomb Taliban targets, America expected a long war. But in just two months, the Northern Alliance and the Pashtuns who opposed the Taliban, backed by American air power and Special Operations forces, defeated the Taliban and took control of the entire country. Obviously, the Taliban's primitive army, which fought from the back of Toyota pickup trucks, was no match for American B-2 stealthbombers and Green Beret soldiers. But the Taliban had also failed to build any loyalty among the Afghan people, who were tired of their repressive rules and cruelty. Usually extremely hostile to outside intervention, many Afghans welcomed American troops into the country. They were hoping the Taliban would be defeated. The majority of Afghans were all too happy to see them fall. With the help of America and the United Nations, the Afghans established a temporary government led by interim leader Hamid Karzai. That government will eventually be replaced by a democratically elected one. But the temporary government does not have secure control over Afghanistan. Many of the temporary government's ministers and provincial governors are the same warlords whose squabbling and fighting originally allowed the Taliban to take power. With much of the Afghan population in refugee camps or suffering from lack of food, Afghanistan faces a long recovery.

Many of the Taliban were captured. Others surrendered their guns and were allowed to return to their villages after pledging loyalty to the new Afghan government. But many Taliban, including Omar, fled into the mountains and hills. There is a danger they may try to regroup and fight America and the new Afghan government.

But in the days after the Taliban lost control, the people rejoiced at the dramatic end to the strict Islamic repression. Many women swapped burqas for simple traditional head scarves. Men lined up at barbershops to shave their beards. Colorful kites and balloons flew over Kabul. Music rang out in Mazar-e-Sharif. When the Taliban had taken power, they had searched for all the television sets in the country and smashed them. Now Afghan men dug up TVs and VCRs they had buried in their backyards. One Afghan popped in a hidden copy of *Titanic* and sat down to watch.

12:00 1:00 2:00 3:00 4:00 5:00 6:00

▼ 12:04 P.M.

Los Angeles International Airport, the intended destination
of three of the crashed planes, is evacuated.

9/11/01

9.
What is
Islamism?

DESPITE THE Taliban's fall from power, al Qaeda is still a dangerous terrorist network with thousands of members scattered in more than sixty countries, ready to launch more attacks on Americans both at home and abroad. After the Taliban fell, the United States government sent military advisers to the countries of the Philippines, Yemen, and Georgia in early 2002 to help those nations fight al Qaeda terrorists and their allies. The FBI and European police began investigating hundreds of al Qaeda members living covertly in Western Europe.

Bin Laden has attracted so many followers from so many different countries because of the deep hatred of America felt by some Muslims. An even larger group of Muslims disapprove of bin Laden's methods but sympathize with his cause and resent America . But what do his followers hope to accomplish if they force America to withdraw from the Muslim world? They hope to replace the governments of their countries, which they see as too corrupt or too Western, with a more Islamic form of government called Islamism. It is a political philosophy which holds wide appeal in the Muslim world.

For the past century, Middle Eastern people who have been dissatisfied with their governments have been divided between two competing political beliefs. Some look at the strength and success of America and say that increased democracy is the answer for the Middle East. If their countries are going to find prosperity in this modern age, they believe they must adopt what they think of as the West's best values—freedom of speech, freedom to choose leaders, freedom to succeed economically. But others look to the Middle East's past for an answer. They believe Muslim nations need to return to the governing principles of the leaders of the great Islamic empires that lasted from 632 to 1919. In those days, they believe, the rulers put Islamic values above all others. Those who hope to apply Islamic values to modern politics are called Islamists. And bin Laden and his followers are the most militant of Islamists—they extol the most strict and conservative Islamic beliefs and believe violence is justified to enforce them. They believe the only way to truly guarantee Islamist governments in Muslim countries is to rid them of all outside influence.

What do Islamists believe?

ISLAMISTS BELIEVE that Muslim nations should look to their religion for political answers. They believe that Islam is not just a faith but a political philosophy for government. In the Qur'an, Muhammad was not just a prophet—he was leader of the community of Medina. He wrote their laws. He sat as judge when people had disputes or someone was accused of having committed a crime. He led the community into battle. It's a striking contrast from the Christianity of the Bible, where Jesus told his followers to leave politics to Caesar and focus instead on their souls. Muhammad's

Afghan men sit on top of a bus in Mazar-e-Sharif, while women sit inside. Islamists believe men and women should be separated in public places.

successors turned his teachings into a set of laws—the sharia. Islamists believe the Qur'an and the sharia should be the law of all Muslim nations. Imagine if the United States' president replaced the Constitution with the New Testament and you begin to get a sense of what Islamists want. Here are some key Islamist beliefs:

■ Islamists believe the sharia should be the basis for laws. Because the Qur'an forbids Muslims to eat pork or drink alcohol, many Islamists believe restaurants and stores should be forbidden to sell pork and alcohol. Because Muslims are not supposed to charge interest when they loan each other money, banks should be forbidden to charge interest on loans. Muslim tradition says women are not supposed to associate with men who aren't family members, to avoid being tempted outside of marriage. Therefore public places should have separate rooms for men and women. There are hundreds more of these rules. Islamists believe religious rules should be law in their countries.

■ Islamists believe the gap between rich and poor must be bridged. Islam teaches that money does not matter to Allah. Islamists want the government to take a more active role in helping the poorer people in their nations. They believe the zakat, the charitable giving required of all Muslims, should be a mandatory tax the government collects and then distributes to Islamic charities. Islamists believe helping the poor should be the first priority of the government. They feel this separates them from Western capitalism, where financial success is often viewed as most important while charity and help for the needy come in a distant second. The U.S. government does try to help the poor, but keeping the economy strong is considered a more urgent goal.

■ Islamists believe Muslim culture must be preserved. In this modern age, when television and billboards bombard Muslim societies with images of Western products and values, Islamists worry their native culture is being replaced with America's. Islamists want their culture protected—their traditional clothing, music, and the Arabic language—even if that means regulating how people dress (especially whether or not women should cover their hair and faces) and banning some Western products and media.

■ Islamists believe their nations need governments like the old Islamic empires'. They insist that these empires endured for more than a thousand years because the government was Islamic and enforced the sharia. And while the ruler then was not democratically elected, he was responsive to the people's desires—listening to a council of men who advised him. Islamists often disagree about what kind of ruler they should have—a king, or a dictator, or a president. But they all agree he must listen to the people's will, and above all, protect the faith.

12:00   1:00   2:00   3:00   4:00   5:00   6:00

▼ 12:15 P.M.

The U.S. announces that its borders with Mexico and Canada have been closed.

9/11/01

■ Islamists believe that if Muslim nations began to return to Islamic principles of government, they could regain their greatness, perhaps even
reunite as an empire once more. To them, this form of government is superior to democracy or any other Western philosophy. They believe Western
ideas like democracy and capitalism are fine for Americans and Europeans,
but not for Muslims. Most Islamists also believe their countries need to be
modernized (the Taliban were a notable exception), but that adopting
Western technology does not mean adopting Western values.

The Islamist desire to recapture the lost glory of the old empires is
slightly misguided, however. Those empires were never as strictly Islamist
as they believe. The leaders were often just as corrupt as modern rulers in

This Qur'an is more than 1,200 years old. Islamists argue that the words of the Qur'an and the
sharia should be enforced as the law of all Muslim nations.

the Middle East. And much of what made the empires great was the rulers' willingness to borrow ideas from the other cultures they encountered. Small nations the Muslims conquered donated their values and traditions to their new rulers. The later caliphs adopted these ideas. They did not rule by the same strict Islamic principles as their predecessors.

How did Islamism start?

THE FIRST Islamists did not focus so much on the past. The philosophy's early scholars actually drew on Western ideas. They started developing their beliefs in the late 1800s, when Europe began to colonize the Middle East. With the empire weakening around them, they wanted to modernize their faith and reenergize it with new ideas. Europe was slowly carving up the Middle East into colonial pieces, and these Islamist scholars wanted to remind all Muslims that they should be united by their common faith, and work together to prevent colonization. But in the last fifty years, as Muslims in the Middle East have grown increasingly frustrated at their countries' problems and the West's dominance, some have made Islamism more radical and more militant, and a few have made it violent. These radicals have come to believe violence is the only way to enact their ideals. They look back to their idealized version of the Islamic empire's past glory. They have also become more rigid, less tolerant of new ideas and dissent.

The first Islamist scholars were actually quite progressive, with plans to modernize Islam. In Egypt during the late 1800s, Islamists began to discuss and develop their ideas. Egypt was already a colony of Great Britain. But several of these scholars actually looked to the West for

12:00 1:00 2:00 3:00 4:00 5:00 6:00

▼ 12:15 P.M.

San Francisco International Airport, the intended destination of flight 93, is evacuated and shut down.

9/11/01
PM

ideas. The most influential was Sayyid Jamal al Din al Afghani, a Persian living in Cairo. He saw Europe's belief in law and justice as the key to a strong, just society. But European states were united by nationalism—the people of each country felt strong ties to their nation because of their shared culture and history. Al Afghani wondered how to adapt Europeans' strong law to the Muslim world, which did not have the same sense of nationalism. Muslims in Morocco had a far different culture and history than Muslims in Indonesia. But they did share a common religion. Al Afghani theorized that Islam and its religious laws could unite Muslim countries the same way that French culture and laws united the people of France.

Still, the Qur'an and sharia discuss laws that applied to life in seventh century Arabia—how could these be adapted to a world of industry, machines, and modern life? Al Afghani studied the Qur'an and discovered several suras that espouse the principle of *ijtihad*, personal reflection on Islam. Ijtihad means that each Muslim should reflect on the words of the Qur'an and interpret the words and actions of Muhammad for himself. It means that the Qur'an doesn't provide instructions for every aspect of life, but by reflecting on Muhammad's principles, each Muslim can decide for himself. Allah gave man the power of thought for a reason. Al Afghani theorized that modern-day Muslims could create new laws for their society based on Islamic ideals. The Qur'an would be their inspiration, but a modern system of law would be their goal.

Al Afghani traveled the world, attempting to teach his ideas to Muslims everywhere. He began publishing a magazine, *Al Urwa al Wuthqa*, which means "The Firm Bond," in 1884. Soon it was read widely by educated Muslims. Al Afghani also wrote to political leaders all over the Middle East, trying to convince them to put his Islamism into practice.

But the leaders ignored him. And al Afghani's ideas were extremely upsetting to the *ulema*, the respected Islamic scholars who taught the faith. They believed Islam was unchanging. No one could change the sharia and hadith that were first written one thousand years earlier. To do so was heresy.

When did Islamism become militant?

DESPITE THE ulema's disapproval, al Afghani's and other Islamists' ideas gained many followers as the Ottoman Empire collapsed in 1919 and the Middle East was colonized by Europe. Middle Eastern Muslims were made to feel like second-class citizens as their European leaders imported their own governments, businesses, and customs. The Europeans told the Muslims this was all for the Muslims' own good—native Middle Eastern practices were too primitive and backward. As Muslim anger grew, Egyptian Hassan al Banna founded the first Islamist political party, the Muslim Brotherhood, in Cairo in 1928. Chapters sprang up throughout the Muslim world made up of members who wanted to rid themselves of European rulers and form Islamist governments.

But as the century wore on, the Islamists had little success changing things, and life didn't improve for Arabs under either European or native rulers. In the 1950s, as Muslims grew more dissatisfied, some Islamists began saying violent revolution against their governments was the only way to get real change. Militant Islamists began assassination attempts and terrorist attacks against Middle Eastern leaders. And as the tension escalated, some Islamists began to agree with the ulema—Islam was strict and unchanging. All traces of modern society and Western values

12:00   1:00   2:00   3:00   4:00   5:00   6:00

▼ 12:36 P.M.

From Barksdale Air Force Base, the president goes on television and says, "Make no mistake, the United States will hunt down and punish those responsible for these cowardly acts."   9/11/01
P.M.

must be destroyed, and Muslim countries must return to an uncompromising, conservative Islamic culture.

Islamists have had some success getting Middle Eastern governments to adopt their ideas. But they have rarely had the sweeping revolutions they wanted. More often, Middle Eastern governments have adopted limited Islamist principles in order to keep their people happy while not giving up an ounce of their power. In 1979, Islamists in Iran won a major victory with the revolution that replaced the shah with a Shi'ite Islamist government. Other Muslim governments have varying degrees of Islamism. Some incorporate sharia into their legal systems, and sometimes Islamic scholars are judges. But most Middle Eastern governments fear Islamist parties. They worry that the more radical parties will try to overthrow them. In many countries, like Morocco, Tunisia, and Egypt, Islamist parties are forbidden. Underground groups still exist, however. And a large portion of the people support at least some Islamism.

What does all this have to do with America?

FOR MOST of the last fifty years, militant Islamists have focused their attacks on their own governments. But the Soviet war changed all that. Most of the Muslims who flocked to Afghanistan to help the mujaheddin were Islamists. They had been resisting their own governments for years. But fighting together in Afghanistan against the Soviets, they realized they were much stronger together. They wanted to work together to bring Islamist governments to all Muslim nations and cleanse those nations of all Western ideals.

Osama bin Laden convinced many of them that the way to truly wake up the Muslim world and force it to embrace Islamism was to launch an all-out war against America. Nothing unites people like a common enemy. Bin Laden hoped that the attacks on September 11th would spur America to declare war on Islam. He hopes that America's attacks on al Qaeda will upset Muslims throughout the world and spark a jihad against the United States. Islamism remains a potent force in the Muslim world, and America must help its Muslim allies give their people a reason to look forward and not back to some idealized Islamist past. September 11th proved that what happens in the Middle East does affect America, and if ignored, it can have deadly results.

12:00   1:00   2:00   3:00   4:00   5:00   6:00

▼ 12:55 P.M.

Taliban officials in Afghanistan deny any responsibility for the attacks.

9/11/01
P.M.

10.
Who is
Osama bin Laden?

IN 1998, Osama bin Laden told ABC News, "In today's wars, there are no morals. We believe the worst thieves in the world today and the worst terrorists are America. We do not have to differentiate between military or civilian. As far as we are concerned, they are all targets."

He is the most infamous terrorist of all time, responsible for the deaths of over four thousand people in the last decade, most of them Americans. Is Osama bin Laden a madman? If he was insane, could he have accomplished such incredible, horrible feats? He has several thousand followers who will continue to believe in his ideals even after he is gone.

He is over six feet four inches tall. He is thin and in recent years has walked with a limp, reportedly from a kidney disease. He is intelligent, quiet, and soft-spoken, even when he is explaining why he believes thousands of people deserve to die. He calmly talked about the twin towers collapse, smiling at the thought of all the people inside. His speech is filled with references to Islam, Allah, and Muhammad. He defines everything he does by his religion, and he uses it to justify all the violence he has committed. As he told one journalist in 1998, "Terrorism can be commendable and it can be reprehensible. The terrorism we practice is the commendable kind for it is directed at the tyrants and the aggressors and the enemies of Allah." Bin Laden began his campaign against America because he believes it is Islam's biggest enemy.

Where did bin Laden come from?

OSAMA BIN LADEN grew up surrounded by wealth and privilege. While bin Laden's story has been an American nightmare, his father's was "the American dream." Mohammed bin Awdah bin Laden emigrated from his

home in Yemen to Saudi Arabia in the early 1900s as a young bricklayer with little money. Within a few decades he was head of the nation's largest construction company and a friend of Saudi king Abdel Aziz ibn Saud. That friendship helped his company, Saudi Bin Laden Group, win a contract to renovate the holy cities of Medina and Mecca, an incredible honor for any Muslim. The bin Laden family has been responsible for all construction inside the holy cities ever since. Today Saudi Bin Laden Group has 35,000 employees worldwide, is worth $5 billion, and is involved in

Osama bin Laden sits during a November 2001 interview with a Pakistani journalist, in an image from a Pakistani daily newspaper, *Dawn*.

many industries besides construction. It has ties to several U.S. companies, bringing products from General Electric to Snapple to Arabia, and it is respected in Europe and America.

Mohammed bin Laden had four wives and fifty-two children, rare for most Arabians but similar to other wealthy or royal families there at that time. A large family was a mark of success. Osama was born in 1957, and Mohammed died just ten years later. Control of the family business was divided up among his older brothers and uncles. Osama inherited $80 million. Invested in Saudi Bin Laden Group, Osama's fortune was estimated to be almost $250 million by the time he was an adult.

How did this wealthy kid end up fighting a terrorist holy war?

BIN LADEN graduated from a Saudi university in 1979 with a degree in civil engineering, a field well suited to working for his family's company. But he had found his real passion while taking an Islamic studies class taught by a professor who inspired him. Dr. Abdullah Azzam was Palestinian and a leading member of the Muslim Brotherhood party. He introduced bin Laden to Islamism. Bin Laden's family had always been religious, but not active in Islamist issues. Now Islamism became bin Laden's passion. When the Soviets invaded Afghanistan in 1979, Azzam and bin Laden, then in his early twenties, eagerly joined the Afghan mujaheddin's efforts to fight back.

Bin Laden was not a soldier. Although there are reports of him taking part in battles in Afghanistan, these were isolated incidents. Because of his personal wealth and his well-known name in the Middle East, he was far more valuable to the mujaheddin as a fundraiser, recruiter, and logistics coordinator. With his vast fortune, bin Laden bought needed construction supplies and medicine and sent them to the mujaheddin. While the United States and other governments were funding some of the mujaheddin groups, Arabs like bin Laden were working to bring more money and supplies to all of them. To help obtain more money and resources, bin Laden and Azzam founded Maktab al Khidmat (MaK), also called the Afghan Bureau. The two men traveled all over the world, visiting mosques and calling on the young men to fight for their faith.

The jihad in Afghanistan transformed bin Laden into a holy warrior. He made valuable contacts with Islamists from all over the world. He developed ties with members of important Islamic charities and learned how they could funnel money to his organization. He saw his efforts help an army of ragtag Muslims defeat a superpower. He felt it was a sign of Allah's power. And he told his supporters that he knew one day they would use that power against America. Despite U.S. support for the Afghans, bin Laden never liked America, blaming it for many of the problems of the Middle East. If the Arab and Afghan mujaheddin could defeat the Soviets, they could defeat the Americans.

Why did bin Laden start al Qaeda?

AT THE end of the Afghan War, bin Laden turned MaK into al Qaeda, which means "the base." The Islamist militants left Afghanistan and began efforts to replace their home countries' governments with Islamist regimes, or to weaken the West. While MaK had been established specifically to help fight the Soviets, Al Qaeda provided money, weapons, and a worldwide support network for the Islamists. Through al Qaeda, bin Laden maintained his contacts with terrorist groups throughout the world.

In 1989 with the war over and international support for the Arab Afghans gone, bin Laden returned home to Saudi Arabia. His mentor, Azzam, was dead, killed by unknown assassins. Bin Laden was looking for a new cause, a new holy war to rally the Muslim world. When Saddam Hussein led an Iraqi invasion into Kuwait and threatened Saudi Arabia itself, bin Laden thought he had found his new fight. He asked the Saudi royal family to let him organize the Arab Afghans to come and defend Saudi Arabia. But they refused his help because they had more powerful allies. Saudi King Fahd invited the Americans and Europeans to Saudi Arabia, the Muslims' sacred kingdom. Bin Laden was outraged. He held America responsible for the Middle East's low status in the world. To have American soldiers walking on Muhammad's ground was an insult to Islam. For his king to ask them for help was too much. Many Saudis felt the same way.

When the Gulf War ended and American soldiers remained in Saudi Arabia, bin Laden began to speak out against King Fahd and the royal family. They were false Muslims, he said, and should be forced out of power. He was exiled in 1992, fleeing to Sudan, which was governed by Hassan al Turabi, a friend from the Afghan war. Because of his disloyalty to the Saudi royal family, bin Laden's own family disowned him soon afterward. While bin Laden was living in Sudan, U.S. troops began a humanitarian mission nearby in the largely Muslim country of Somalia. But when eighteen American soldiers were killed in a furious battle in 1993—the first casualties of the conflict—America withdrew from the war-torn nation. America's quick retreat convinced bin Laden that America was

Bin Laden's top men

AL QAEDA'S leadership has the same alliance structure as the rest of the net-work–Bin Laden's chief lieutenants are from different countries and organizations. Ayman al Zawahiri, an Egyptian, is in charge of al Qaeda ideology–he writes pamphlets and books explaining al Qaeda's beliefs and why all Muslims should join its jihad. Al Zawahiri is a fifty-year-old trained surgeon who grew up in a wealthy Egyptian family, but gave it up for a life of terror early on. He was a leading figure in an Islamist terror organization and was involved in the 1981 assassination of Egyptian president Anwar Sadat. Al Zawahiri was arrested after the assassination and spent several years in prison. He joined bin Laden in Afghanistan in 1996. One year later, Egypt convicted him of various charges and sentenced him to death if he ever returns. Al Zawahiri has been described as a humble, charismatic leader by some who have worked with him, but also as a cruel man who has executed colleagues and their family members for betraying him.

Mohammed Atef, once an Egyptian policeman, was in charge of organizing al Qaeda attacks until he was killed by a U.S. bomb in Afghanistan the November after 9/11. His successor was Abu Zubaydah, a thirty-year-old Palestinian who grew up in Saudi Arabia. For several years, Zubaydah was in charge of screening potential recruits before they were sent to training camps in Afghanistan. Once their training was complete, Zubaydah assigned them their missions. Zubaydah has traveled extensively to coordinate future attacks, using numerous false identities. He is incredibly dangerous because he is one of the few people who knows the identity of the thousands of al Qaeda members throughout the world and could dispatch them on new terror attacks. Zubaydah was arrested while hiding in Pakistan in March 2002 by Pakistani authorities with American help. U.S. intelligence hopes to learn al Qaeda members' identities by questioning Zubaydah. But al Qaeda's leadership is large, and undoubtedly a new operations chief will emerge.

12:00 1:00 2:00 ▼ 2:44 P.M. 3:00 4:00 5:00 6:00

Five warships leave the U.S. Naval Station in Norfolk, Virginia, to protect the east coast from further attack.

9/11/01
P.M.

weak and cowardly. He began to organize a terrorist campaign against the superpower.

After the U.S. fled Somalia, bin Laden began to urge all al Qaeda-supported terrorists to attack the U.S. He set up terrorist training camps in Sudan and Yemen. In 1995, five Americans were killed in a truck bombing in Saudi Arabia. The terrorists told Saudi authorities that bin Laden had inspired them. The U.S. and Saudi Arabia pressured Sudan to kick bin Laden out. Forced to leave in 1996, bin Laden returned to Afghanistan, where the Taliban welcomed him and the money he gave them to help fight their war. Shortly afterward, he issued a *fatwa*, a public declaration of jihad, against the U.S. Normally only a religious leader, an imam or mullah, can issue such a declaration. But by then bin Laden saw himself as the Muslim world's hero and felt it was his duty to declare the fatwa. A few mullahs denounced what he did, but bin Laden was more concerned with winning the support of the average Muslim. The fatwa worked. Many Muslims began to sympathize with his cause. New recruits came to his new training camps in Afghanistan to learn how to wage jihad for al Qaeda.

How is al Qaeda structured?

BIN LADEN'S secret to creating the most powerful terrorist group ever is al Qaeda's structure. Just as his father's company became a multinational conglomerate—a combination of smaller companies—al Qaeda is an alliance of smaller terrorist groups in more than sixty different countries. Bin Laden used the contacts he had made in Afghanistan to bring various Islamist militant groups together. Each of these groups has its own local agenda, but all are part of al Qaeda and carry out missions for bin Laden. In return, bin Laden provides money and support.

While bin Laden lived in Afghanistan, any Islamist terrorist who wanted to could train in camps there, learning sabotage, urban warfare, explosives, and how to blend in while living in Western countries. Al Qaeda members wrote lengthy manuals on terror and distributed them throughout the world on paper and CD-ROMs. After training, individual al Qaeda cells were dispatched to carry out missions. Once hidden in their target country, they were financed with organization money or committed petty crimes like burglary or credit-card fraud to earn cash. Because al Qaeda cells were in so many countries, bin Laden was able to attack the U.S. on several different fronts. When bombers attacked the U.S.S. *Cole* in Yemen, a cell of Yemenis carried out the attack. A cell of Algerians were planning the millennium bombings of Los Angeles Airport and Jordanian tourist sites before authorities stopped them. The September 11th attacks were launched by men from five different countries.

Even before America attacked Afghanistan, bin Laden's life there was not easy. He moved nightly to avoid American attempts to find him, living mostly in the Afghan countryside, but occasionally visiting Kandahar or his terrorist camps. His four wives and more than ten children followed him. After the 9/11

The port side of the U.S.S. *Cole* was damaged after a suspected terrorist bomb exploded during a refueling operation in October 2000 in Aden, Yemen.

12:00 1:00 2:00 3:00 ▼ 2:50 P.M. 4:00 5:00 6:00

The president arrives at Offutt Air Force Base in Nebraska. He teleconferences with the eight-member National Security Council.

9/11/01

attacks, bin Laden's efforts to evade detection became even more intense. But he continued to release videotaped messages calling on Muslims to rise up and kill Americans. Bin Laden hoped America would be just as frightened of losing soldiers in Afghanistan as it had been in Somalia. He hoped that his attacks and an ineffective U.S. retaliation would prove America was weak and drive Muslims into a worldwide holy war. But America was able to defeat the Taliban. And Muslims did not rise up in a holy war. Many were horrified by the 9/11 attacks. Others saw bin Laden run and hide from the Americans and decided he was not as strong as he claimed to be.

What happens if bin Laden is captured or killed?

IT WOULD be very dangerous for America to think it has won the war against terrorism just by capturing or killing bin Laden. He may already be dead. However, al Qaeda members, as many as 10,000 by some estimates, are still at large throughout the world. Rooting them out will involve law enforcement, espionage, and diplomacy. American intelligence agencies have been working with allies overseas. For example, with American help Singapore police caught an al Qaeda cell plotting a new bombing attack. The U.S. faces years of similar efforts at home and abroad before al Qaeda is destroyed.

11.
How has America changed since September 11th?

SEPTEMBER 11th, 2001, is now a part of American history, as well known as the day Pearl Harbor was attacked, or the Civil War began, or the Declaration of Independence was signed. We are living in historical times, which is not always easy, but it is important to know that how we react to the attacks will determine the future of our nation and the world. Ultimately you'll help decide how the attacks shape that future. How did they change the nation in the first months afterward?

We were united by patriotism.

AMERICA HAS always thrived on being a country that celebrates differences. Just looking at the faces of those who died that horrible day reminds us that every kind of person, regardless of race or religion, is welcome here in America. But sometimes those differences make us feel divided from one another. And before 9/11, Americans rarely focused on patriotism. When our lives are spent worrying about the smaller things, and when our democracy seems centered on petty politics, we can forget how great this country can be. Before 9/11, how many Americans didn't think much when they looked at the flag or heard the national anthem at a ball game?

But September 11th reminded us how special this country is and how much we share. Within hours after the attacks, Americans were united by patriotism and by a strong desire to help. Stores sold out of flags within a few days as everyone hung the Stars and Stripes to show that they still believed in America. At baseball games everyone stood to sing "The Star-Spangled Banner" and "God Bless America." And the differences that sometimes divided us didn't seem as important for a while. We were all Americans.

We reached out to help one another.

IN THE hours and days after 9/11, people wanted desperately to help. Rescue crews and ordinary people from all over the country drove around the clock to reach New York and lend a hand in recovery efforts at the site where the twin towers fell, now called Ground Zero. The city eventually had to turn volunteers away, there were so many. Money poured into charities, as Americans both rich and poor gave whatever they could to help the victims and their families. And countries around the world felt Americans' pain. In England, in Germany, in Japan, all over the world, people sang "The Star-Spangled Banner" to show their solidarity.

Before 9/11, we often looked for people to blame for our problems. After the attacks, while many asked who was responsible for such a horrible crime, almost everyone also looked for the heroes. People wanted to know that even though some misguided men filled with hate had done this, others—many others—were showing how good and unselfish people could be. Americans everywhere paid tribute to the passengers of flight 93 who had stopped the hijackers on their plane. These passengers had known the plane would probably go down and they would all most likely die, but they successfully prevented the terrorists from killing anyone else on the ground. And countless tributes were paid to the rescue workers—the police and firefighters who ran into the World Trade Center to help people get out. New York City's mayor Rudolph Giuliani,

Rescuers evacuate a victim of the September 11th attacks in New York City.

who spoke at many of the funerals for the 343 firefighters who died, often said that at the moment the terrorists attacked, they failed. When brave Americans ran into those towers, they showed that they would not be scared into submission. They would risk their lives to help each other.

Americans also began to look overseas to help the people of

12:00   1:00   2:00   3:00   4:00   5:00   6:00

▼ 4:00 P.M.

U.S. officials announce that they suspect Osama bin Laden is involved in the attacks.   9/11/01 P.M.

Afghanistan. It would have been easy to blame the Afghan people for 9/11. Instead, we realized that they were victims too, and began to donate food, money, and more to help them rebuild their country.

We were filled with suspicion and fear.

IN THE aftermath of the attacks, the entire country was filled with fear. America had rarely been attacked by overseas forces, and never on such a large scale. Suddenly we were no longer safe here. No one was sure what would happen next. Would the terrorists strike again, and how? Would they try attacks with biological or chemical weapons? In the following months, several people became ill and a few died of anthrax poisoning after handling letters contaminated by the bacteria. The fear increased.

In times of fear, it's normal to look for someone to blame. Unfortunately, in the months after September 11th, some Americans looked to their Middle Eastern and Muslim neighbors. A gas station owner was shot dead because he was wearing a turban. There were other isolated attacks on Muslims. But when the president addressed the nation two weeks after the 11th, he called on Americans not to resort to violence and prejudice. Fear and hate are the very fuel that Osama bin Laden tapped when he created al Qaeda and began his terrorist campaign. American Muslims are Americans, too. And by living here, they prove that the United States is not an enemy of Islam.

Some suspicions did linger. The Justice Department, working hard to prevent future attacks, tried to limit some civil liberties—the legal rights all Americans enjoy. A majority of Americans have felt that some limited restrictions on civil liberties were acceptable in a time of danger. Federal agents began holding Muslim immigrants on minor charges and refusing to release their names to the public. This made it difficult for their families and lawyers to help them. The Justice Department also discussed trying suspected terrorists in front of military tribunals instead of regular courts. A military court would give the accused fewer rights—denying them the right to a trial in front of a jury, for example. Attorney General John Ashcroft even told Congress that anyone who questioned the Department's actions was helping the terrorists.

Nothing could be further from the truth. The Justice Department's success has been limited so far. Thankfully, America is not giving up the civil liberties it believes in. But we need to be careful. Questioning actions like the Justice Department's is what America is all about. Every individual has the right to question, to speak out, to make sure their rights are safe. Democracy is about participation. We cannot throw out the Constitution that makes this nation so special, that protects people from an oversuspicious government, at the very moment we are being attacked. Giving up some civil liberties could lead to giving up more and more. It would be admitting the terrorists are right, that our nation isn't the strong democracy we think it is.

We realized we had a role to play in the world.

AMERICA HAS always been a reluctant superpower. Throughout history we have looked at the messy affairs of the world and often decided we would rather not get involved unless we have to. In the months before the attacks, for example, President Bush refused to try to negotiate

12:00   1:00   2:00   3:00   4:00   ▼ 4:10 P.M.   5:00   6:00

Building 7 of the World Trade Center complex is reported to be on fire.   9/11/01 P.M.

U.S. secretary of state Colin Powell (right) shakes hands with Afghanistan's interim leader Hamid Karzai at the presidential palace in Kabul, January 17, 2002.

peace between Israel and the Palestinians. Tensions grew in the Middle East as the two sides fought. September 11th taught us we cannot escape the rest of the world. What happens in another part of the world can have drastic effects here at home. In March 2002, Bush began a renewed effort at peace in Israel, partially to improve relations between America and the Middle East.

In 1989, when the Soviet Union pulled its troops out of Afghanistan, the U.S. ended its involvement in the war-torn nation. We had only been concerned with stopping the Soviets' advance. But our withdrawal left

Afghanistan to endless misery. We were not solely responsible, but we could have made a difference if we had tried to bring peace to Afghanistan after helping fight a war there. This time, we are trying. The Taliban has fallen, and America and the United Nations are helping establish a unified, peaceful government for the Afghan people and sending humanitarian aid. By working with the Afghan people, U.S. troops are able to continue looking for members of al Qaeda inside Afghanistan. And by staying involved for a long time, we can help ensure the Taliban does not regain power. It can be frustrating. Afghanistan needs a lot of help. An entire generation knows nothing but violence. Their country is in physical and economic ruins. Millions of people have lost their homes and are refugees. There will be setbacks, but by playing an active role the U.S. can help shape the future.

What can *you* do?

YOU CAN learn about other countries and cultures. Read books to find out more about the topics covered in this book. Follow the news both here and overseas on TV and in magazines and newspapers. Ask your teachers lots of questions. Try to understand what it's like to see the world through the eyes of someone in another country. Learn other languages, and about foreign food, art, and literature. If we only focus on ourselves and what goes on within our borders, we have no understanding of or control over what happens overseas. Terrorism will have a free hand. Understanding people's beliefs and religion shows them that you value them. And it can prevent misunderstandings and anger. Think about all the resentment of America around the world. Much of it could be prevented if people who

12:00   1:00   2:00   3:00   4:00   5:00   6:00

▼ 5:20 P.M.

Building 7 of the World Trade Center complex collapses.
The building had already been evacuated.
9/11/01

hated America truly understood what we believe. And much of it could be prevented if we understood their values and respected them more, and if we didn't ignore the problems of the outside world. Those are America's problems, too. There will always be people like Osama bin Laden who will find an excuse to hate America. And the world is a small place nowadays. A few men like bin Laden can engineer horrible violence like the attacks on America. But a nation like America can have a powerful effect on the rest of the world. Without the widespread dislike of America in the Muslim world, bin Laden would have little support for his violence.

You can also resolve never to forget 9/11. Think about what would be the best way to honor those who died that day. You could organize a memorial or a tribute on the anniversary. Or you could honor their memories by doing something to prevent another 9/11. Teach others what you know. Or coordinate a community action that will promote peace in the Middle East or anywhere in the world. Raise money for children in a struggling nation like Afghanistan. And keep 9/11 fresh in people's minds. Barely six months after the attacks, America was already turning toward concerns besides terrorism. It's important that we move on and deal with other problems. But if we forget about 9/11, we will lose sight of all we learned from that horrible day. We will never forget the thousands who died that day, but we must remember the lessons we learned from it as well, so that there will not be another September 11th.

Acknowledgments

I WAS A LITTLE nervous when I agreed to write this book, my first, but I didn't know then what a great group of people would be helping me. I want to thank Jill Davis, Tracy Gates, and Catherine Frank for being patient, smart, supportive, and tireless editors. I also want to thank Janet Pascal, Nancy Brennan, Teresa Kietlinski, Regina Hayes, and all the other people at Viking for all their work. Also thanks to Resat Kasaba and Daniel Davis.

I'm lucky to have great coworkers at *Time* who let me take on this project and made all the hours covering this horrible story worth it. Thanks to Jim Kelly, Eric Pooley, and Ratu Kamlani for their support and patience.

Any experienced author might warn you it's not smart to let your wife edit your book. They would be wrong. Catherine, thank you so much for being my partner, teacher, cheerleader, and friend. I could not have done this without you.

Glossary

AL QAEDA: The terrorist network started by Osama bin Laden in Afghanistan. It means "the base" in Arabic.

AYMAN AL ZAWAHIRI: al Qaeda's second-in-command; an Egyptian doctor who is in charge of ideology for the terrorist network.

ALLAH: Arabic word for God, or "the One." The term is used by Arabic Christians as well as Muslims.

AMIR: Arabic for "commander." Caliphs were also known as Amirs ul Momineen, or "Commanders of the Faithful"; the Taliban's leader, Mohammed Omar, gave himself the title Amir ul Momineen.

OSAMA BIN LADEN: A wealthy Saudi terrorist, founder and leader of al Qaeda; dedicated to waging a war of terror against the U.S. in an effort to drive America out of the Middle East.

BURQA: A traditional garment that covers the entire body including hands and feet with only a tiny mesh screen to see out of; worn by many women in Afghanistan, Pakistan, and some other Muslim nations.

CALIPH: A position created after Muhammad's death to provide a political leader for the Muslims. At first, former advisers to the prophet held the position. Later, it became a hereditary title, like king. The position was largely replaced by the sultan in the thirteenth century.

CLERIC: a religious official or leader.

COLD WAR: The ideological struggle between the Soviet Union and the United States that began shortly after the end of World War II and continued for more than four decades. Instead of fighting each other in a direct or "hot" war, which could lead to nuclear war, the two nations fought by trying to gain influence over other nations and to spread their competing political beliefs: communism and democracy.

COMMUNISM: An ideology of government and economics that says all property should be collectively owned; the first communist government ruled in the Soviet Union.

FATWA: An Islamic rule or pronouncement issued by a cleric or scholar.

HADITH: Sayings and actions of Muhammad. Muslims view them as a guide to how to live the ideal Islamic life.

HAJJ: The pilgrimage by Muslims to Mecca for days of prayer and ritual; every Muslim is required to make the trip, if possible, at least once.

HEZBOLLAH: Arabic for "Party of God." Hezbollah (sometimes spelled Hizballah) is a Shi'ite Islamist political party and terrorist organization based in Lebanon and Syria. Members want to turn Lebanon into an Islamist state like Iran, and to destroy Israel.

IDEOLOGY: A set of beliefs based on certain ideas about politics, society, and culture.

IDOLATRY: Worshipping a physical object, such as a statue or painting, as a god. Strictly forbidden in Islam, Christianity, and Judaism. Islam and Judaism consider any religious use of representative art idolatry.

IJTIHAD: Arabic for "individual reasoning." In Islam it means that each Muslim has the right to interpret the faith's teachings.

IMAM: In Sunni Islam, a group prayer leader in a mosque or gathering of Muslims. In Shi'ite Islam, the spiritual leader of a community.

INFIDEL: Someone who doesn't believe in a particular religion. To Christians, infidels don't believe in Christianity; to Muslims, infidels don't believe in Islam.

ISLAM: The religious faith of one billion people throughout the world. Arabic for "submission (to God)," Islam is based on the teachings of Muhammad, who lived in Arabia in the seventh century.

ISLAMISM: A political belief that government and laws should be based on Islamic principles.

JIHAD: Arabic for "striving for Islam"; also defined as holy war. The Qur'an urges Muslims to wage jihad for their faith. Some interpret that as striving to be the best Muslim possible and defending the faith. Others believe it means actually waging war for the faith.

JIHADI: Someone fighting a holy war for Islam.

HAMID KARZAI: Leader of the provincial Afghan government established after the Taliban were overthrown in 2001; Karzai's father was a respected Pashtun tribal leader; Karzai led a band of Pashtun rebels against the Taliban with U.S. help.

AYATOLLAH RUHOLLAH KHOMEINI: Iranian cleric and revolutionary who founded a Shi'ite Islamist government during the 1979 revolution in Iran.

MADRASSAH: An Islamic religious school.

MAKTAB AL KHIDMAT (MAK): The "Afghan Bureau"; an organization founded by Osama bin Laden and Abdullah Azzam during the war between the Soviets and Afghans in 1984. It provided money and guns to the Afghan mujaheddin and recruited Muslims from around the world to fight the Soviets.

AHMED SHAH MASSOUD: One of Afghanistan's most legendary mujaheddin, he was part of the ill-fated government founded in Kabul after the Soviets withdrew. Known as the Lion of Panjshir Valley, he fought the Taliban until al Qaeda assassins fatally wounded him on September 9, 2001.

MECCA: City in Saudi Arabia where Muhammad was born and began preaching. It is Islam's holiest city, where Muslim pilgrims on the hajj come.

MEDINA: Islam's second holiest city. It is north of Mecca in Saudi Arabia. Muhammad governed the city during the last ten years of his life and died there.

MONOTHEISM: A religious belief in one God and no other deities. The world's major monotheistic religions are Christianity, Islam, and Judaism.

MOSQUE: An Islamic house of worship where Muslims pray. Also called a masjid.

MUHAMMAD: Arab religious leader who lived in the seventh century. Muslims believe he founded Islam in 610 and is God's final prophet. He died in 632.

MUJAHEDDIN: One who strives for Islam, usually someone who wages a jihad.

MULLAH: An Islamic scholar who teaches others about the faith and is seen as a source of wisdom and advice.

MUSLIM: A person who believes in Islam.

PALESTINIAN LIBERATION ORGANIZATION: (PLO): Terrorist organization begun by Yasser Arafat devoted to obtaining a homeland for the Palestinian people.

POLITICAL COUP: The overthrow of a government by rebellious members, such as cabinet ministers or military officers.

QUR'AN: The religious book of Islam. Muslims believe God recited the book to Muhammad, who repeated it to his followers.

RAMADAN: Month on the Islamic calendar during which Muslims pray and fast daily from sunrise to sunset.

SHAHADA: When a person becomes a Muslim, surrendering to God by announcing there is one God and Muhammad was his prophet.

SHARIA: A code of laws and moral guidelines governing Muslims based on Islamic teachings including the Qur'an and the hadith.

SHI'ITES: Members of the Shia sect of Islam; they believe their spiritual leader should be an Imam directly descended from Muhammad and his cousin Ali.

SUFIS: Members of a sect of Islam that explores the faith's more mystical side, often using song and dance to try and connect with God.

SUNNIS: Muslims from the largest and original sect of Islam, roughly 85 percent of Muslims.

SURAS: Chapters in the Qur'an.

TALIBAN: Arabic for "students of Islam," it is also the name of the militantly Islamist group that ruled Afghanistan from 1996 to 2001. An individual student is called a talib.

TERRORIST: Someone who uses violence to frighten others in order to achieve a political agenda.

ULEMA: Senior Islamic scholars; they are often viewed as the chief leaders of Islam.

UMMA: Arabic for the community of Muslims; all Muslims worldwide.

WAHHABISM: An offshoot of Sunnism, this movement seeks to get back to the basics of Islam. It began and is largely practiced in Saudi Arabia.

WARLORD: A military leader who rules a territory by force.

ZAKAT: A mandatory donation all Muslims must give to charity; one of the five pillars of Islam.

Bibliography

CHAPTER 1

Gibbs, Nancy, and the staff of *Time*. "Day of Infamy." *Time*, September 12, 2001.

Johnson, Glen. "Fighting Terror." *The Boston Globe*, November 23, 2001.

Schultz, Marisa. "Teachers, Pupils Slain in Crash Honored." *The Los Angeles Times*, November 8, 2001.

CHAPTER 2

Cloud, John. "Atta's Odyssey." *Time*, October 8, 2001.

Cloud, John, with reporting by Elaine Shannon. "The Plot Comes into Focus." *Time*, October 1, 2001.

McGeary, Johanna, and David Van Biema. "The New Breed of Terrorist." *Time*, September 24, 2001.

CHAPTER 3

Belt, Don, editor. *National Geographic: The World of Islam*. Washington, D.C.: National Geographic, 2001.

Coogan, Tim Pat. *The Troubles*. London: Palgrave, 2002.

Curtius, Mary. "Bomb Kills 16 in Jerusalem Pizzeria." *The Los Angeles Times*, August 10, 2001.

Elliott, Marianne. *The Catholics of Ulster: A History*. New York: Basic Books, 2001.

Harrison, Eric, and Melissa Healy. "2 Blasts Hit Atlanta Abortion Clinic." *The Los Angeles Times*, January 17, 1997.

Jacquard, Roland. "The Guidebook of Jihad." *Time*, October 29, 2001.

Jenkins, Brian M. "The Organization Men." In *How Did This Happen? Terrorism and the New War*, edited by James F. Hoge Jr. and Gideon Rose. New York: Public Affairs, 2001.

Miller, Marjorie. "Worst Bombing in Northern Ireland Conflict Kills at Least 28." *The Los Angeles Times*, August 16, 1998.

Scherman, Rabbi Nosson, and Rabbi Meir Zlotowitz, editors. *History of the Jewish People: The Second Temple Era*. Brooklyn: Mesorah Publications Ltd., 1982.

Simon, Jeffrey D. *The Terrorist Trap*. Bloomington: Indiana University Press, 2001.

CHAPTER 4

Armstrong, Karen. "Was It Inevitable—Islam through History." In *How Did This Happen? Terrorism and the New War*, edited by James F. Hoge Jr. and Gideon Rose. New York: Public Affairs, 2001.

Beyer, Lisa. "The Women of Islam." *Time*, December 3, 2001.

Farah, Dr. Caesar E. *Islam*. Hauppauge, N.Y.: Barron's Educational Series, Inc., 2000.

The Holy Qur'an. Translation by Abdullah Yusuf Ali. Elmhurst, N.Y.: Tahrike Tarsile Qur'an, Inc., 2001.

Lewis, Bernard. *The Middle East*. New York: Scribner, 1995.

Lippman, Thomas W. *Understanding Islam*. New York: Meridian, 1995.
Rushdie, Salman. "A War That Presents All of Us with a Crisis of Faith." *The Guardian*, November 3, 2001.

CHAPTER 5

Belt, Don, editor. *National Geographic: The World of Islam*. Washington, D.C.: National Geographic, 2001.
Beyer, Lisa. "Roots of Rage." *Time*, October 1, 2001.
Lewis, Bernard. *The Middle East*. New York: Scribner, 1995.
MacLeod, Scott. "Inside Saudi Arabia." *Time*, October 15, 2001.

CHAPTER 6

Associated Press. "Israel's Wars—And How They Ended." April 5, 2002.
Belt, Don, editor. *National Geographic: The World of Islam*. Washington, D.C.: National Geographic, 2001.
Lewis, Bernard. *The Middle East*. New York: Scribner, 1995.
Lewis, Bernard. "The Revolt of Islam." *The New Yorker*, November 19, 2001.

CHAPTER 7

Belt, Don, editor. *National Geographic: The World of Islam*. Washington, D.C.: National Geographic, 2001.
Huband, Mark. *Warriors of the Prophet: The Struggle For Islam*. Boulder, Colo.: Westview Press, 1999.
Lewis, Bernard. *The Middle East*. New York: Scribner, 1995.
Rashid, Ahmed. *Taliban*. New Haven, Conn.: Yale University Press, 2001.

CHAPTER 8

Gibbs, Nancy. "Blood and Joy." *Time*, November 26, 2001.
Rashid, Ahmed. *Taliban*. New Haven, Conn.: Yale University Press, 2001.

CHAPTER 9

Huband, Mark. *Warriors of the Prophet: The Struggle for Islam*. Boulder, Colo.: Westview Press, 1999.
Lippman, Thomas W. *Understanding Islam*. New York: Meridian, 1995.
Rushdie, Salman. "A War That Presents All of Us with a Crisis of Faith." *The Guardian*, November 3, 2001.

CHAPTER 10

Belt, Don, editor. *National Geographic: The World of Islam*. Washington, D.C.: National Geographic, 2001.
Eisenberg, Daniel. "Osama's Top Brass." *Time*, October 8, 2001.
Elliott, Michael. "Hate Club." *Time*, November 12, 2001.
Rashid, Ahmed. *Taliban*. New Haven, Conn.: Yale University Press, 2001.
Shadid, Anthony. "Network Rooted in 1970s Egypt." *The Boston Globe*, October 29, 2001.

CHAPTER 11

Van Biema, David. "As American as . . ." *Time*, October 1, 2001.

Index

Numbers in italic indicate illustrations.

Afghanistan, 72–83, *75*
    as base for Al Qaeda, 72, 84
    ethnic groups in, 73–74, 81, 90, 91
    facts about, 81
    life in, 82–83
    location and geography of, 73–76
    opium crop, 84
    rebuilding of, 119–20, 123
    Soviet involvement in, 32, 76–82, 110, 111, 122
    after Soviet withdrawal, 80–82, 84–85, 90
    Taliban rule of, 72, 84–97
    warlords in, 81–82, 84
al Afghani, Sayyid Jamal al Din, 104–105, *105*
al Banna, Hassan, 105
al Ghamdi, Ahmed, 17
al Ghamdi, Hamza, 17
al Ghamdi, Saeed, 17
al Hazmi, Nawaf, 17, 23
al Hazmi, Salem, 17, 23
al Haznawi, Ahmad, 17
al Midhar, Khalid, 17
al Nami, Ahmed, 17
al Omari, Abdulaziz, 17, 23
al Qadi Banihammad, Fayez Ahmed, 17
al Qaeda, 17, 18, 21, 23, 71, 107
    alliance with Taliban against Northern Alliance, 95
    as continuing threat, 99, 116, 123
    differences from other terrorist groups, 33–35
    founding of, 32, 72, 83, 111–14
    goals of, 33, 111–12
    history of terrorist activities of, 33–35
    leadership, 113
    religious motivations, 18, 23, 33, 36–37
    structure of, 114–16

    training camps, 72, 84, 114, 115
    see also bin Laden, Osama
al Shehhi, Marwan, 6, 17, 20, 22
al Shehri, Mohand, 17
al Shehri, Wail, 17
al Shehri, Waleed, 17
al Turabi, Hassan, 112
Al Urwa al Wuthqa, 104
al Zawahiri, Ayman, 113
Alexander the Great, 73
anthrax, 25, 120
Arab Afghans, 80, 83, 95, 106–107, 112
    after Soviet withdrawal from Afghanistan, 80–81
    exiled from their native countries, 81
Ashcroft, John, 121
Atta, Mohammed, 5–6, 17, 18–20, 21–22, 23
Atef, Mohammed, 113
Azzam, Dr. Abdullah, 110, 111, 112

Bahrain, 66
Bamian, Afghanistan, 91
bin Laden, Mohammed bin Awdah, 109, 110
bin Laden, Osama, 17–18, 23, 32, 36, 49, 51, 71, 107–16, *109*
    background of, 109–10
    exiled from Saudi Arabia and Sudan, 95
    as leader of Arab Afghans, 80
    Mullah Omar and, 95
    Taliban and, 95, 114
    taped messages, 60, 62, 110
    transformation of, 110–11
    see also al Qaeda
biological weapons, 15, 25
Black September, 28
Boutros-Ghali, Boutros, 83
burqas, 43, *43*, 94, *94*, 97
Bush, George H. W., 70
Bush, George W., 11–12, 65, 121–22

caliph, 46
Carter, Jimmy, 65
Central Intelligence Agency (CIA), 14, 35
        aid to mujaheddin of Afghanistan, 77–78
chemical weapons, 15
Christianity, 49–50, 52
        prosperity of Christian Europe, 61
civil liberties, 120–21
Cold War, 64–66, 70
        Soviet and U.S. involvement in Afghanistan and,
        76–83, 122–23
Cole, U.S.S., 34, 115, 115
communism, 64–65, 66
Crusades, 49–50

Defense Intelligence Agency (DIA), 35
Deobandi Islam, 86–87
Dome of the Rock, 52, 53

Egypt, 58, 62, 65, 66
Empire State Building, 2
Encyclopedia of Jihad, 34
Europe, prosperity of, 61

Fahd, King, 112
fatalities, September 11th, 5, 10, 12–13
fatwa, 114
fear:
        after 9/11, 120–21
        as goal of terrorism, 16, 24–25
Federal Bureau of Investigation (FBI), 14, 17, 21, 99
firefighters, 8, 12–13, 119

Genghis Khan, 73
Georgia, 99, 116
Giuliani, Rudolph, 119
Gulf War, 56, 57, 68–70, 112

hadith, 44–45
Hanjour, Hani, 17, 22
Hazaras, 74, 91
Henry, Emile, 25
Hezbollah, 32
hijab, 43
hijacked airplanes, 5–8, 12, 119

hijackers, terrorist, 5–6, 17, 18, 19, 19, 22
        activities in America, 20–23
hospitals, 4, 10, 13
Hussein, Saddam, 56, 68–70, 112

ibn Saud, King Abdel Aziz, 109
ijtihad, 104
India, 37
Indonesia, 37
Inter-Services Intelligence (ISI), Pakistan, 77–78
Iqbal, Mohammed, 73
Iran, 67–68, 69, 85, 91, 106
Iraq, 56, 68–70, 112
Irish Republican Army (IRA), 30–31, 33
Islam (Muslims), 36–50
        in Afghanistan, 73–74
        beliefs, 38–40, 42–43, 47, 48, 63, 71
        empire, 45–48, 46, 61, 100, 101, 102–103
        extremists, 18, 23, 33, 36–37, 38, 49, 50, 71, 86–88
        pilgrimage to Mecca (hajj), 36, 39–40, 53–56
        Qur'an, see Qur'an
        resentment of the United States, see resentment of the
                United States in the Middle East
        splits within, 47–48
        spread of, 45–48
        Taliban's interpretation of, 86–88
        treatment of American Muslims after 9/11, 120–21
        values, 63, 100
        women, beliefs toward, 42–43, 100
Islamism and Islamists, 99–107, 110, 111
        beginnings of, 103–105
        beliefs of, 45, 99–103
        impact on America, 106–107
        militancy of, 105–106
        mujaheddin groups in Afghanistan, 78, 106
        in Pakistan, 78
        Taliban, see Taliban
Israel, 122
        American support for, 57, 61, 65, 70
        peace treaties with Arab neighbors, 65
        terrorism in, 24, 27–29, 31, 53

Jamiat e Ulema Islam, 87
Jarrah, Ziad Samir, 17, 18, 20
Jerusalem, Israel, 52–53, 53
jihad, 48–50, 71, 90, 107, 111

jihadis, 80
Jordan, 58
Judaism, 52, 53
Justice Department, U.S., 120–21

Kabul, Afghanistan, 90–91
Kabul University, 93
Kandahar Province, Afghanistan, 85, 86, 95
Karzai, Hamid, 96, *122*
Kashmir, 80
Khomeini, Ayatollah Ruhollah, 68, *69*
Kikmetyar, Gulbuddin, 81
Koran, *see* Qur'an
Kuwait, 56, 57, 68, 70, 112

Lebanon, 32
Loya Jirga, 76

McVeigh, Timothy, 14
madrassahs, 80, 85, 87, 89
Maktab al Khidmat (MaK), 110–11
marketing of American products in the Middle East, 62
Massoud, Ahmed Shah, 90, 91, 95–96
Mazar-e-Sharif, Afghanistan, 91, 97
Mecca, 36, *39*, 39–40, 53–56
Medina, 41, 53
Middle East, 51–59, *54*
    economic importance of, 51, 56–59
    Islamism in, *see* Islamism and Islamists
    map of, 54–55
    peace negotiations, 65, 121–22
    political instability of, 51, 59
    poverty in, 58–59, 61–62
    religious importance of, 51, 52–56
    repressive governments in, 58, 59, 61, 66
    resentment of the United States in, *see* resentment of
        the United States in the Middle East
Moqed, Majed, 17, *22*
Moussaoui, Zacarias, 21
Muhammad, 37, 40–41, 44, 45, 49, 52, 53, 90, 99
mujaheddin, 77, 90, 110–11
    Arab Afghans, *see* Arab Afghans
    composition of, 79–80
    defeat of Afghan communist government, 81
    Taliban composed of former, 84
mullahs, 38, 114

Munich Olympics, 28
Muslims, *see* Islam (Muslims)
Northern Alliance, 91, 95, 96
Northern Ireland, terrorism and, 24, 27, 29–31
nuclear weapons, 15

oil, Middle Eastern, 51, 56–59, 61
Oklahoma City, terrorist attack in, 14
Oman, 66
Omar, Mullah Mohammed, 85, 86, 87, 89, *89*, 90, 91, 96–97
    bin Laden and, 95
OPEC, 58
Oslo Accord, 1993, 65

Pahlavi, Shah Mohammed Reza, 67–68
Pakistan, 37, 77–78, 85, 86, 87, 113
    involvement in Afghan war against the Soviet Union,
        77–78, 79–80
    Taliban takeover of Afghanistan and, 88–89
Palestinian Liberation Organization (PLO), 28–29, 31
Palestinians, 24, 27–29, 33, 53, 65, 70, *122*
Pashtuns, 74, 78, 87, 89, 90, 96
patriotism, 117–18
Pearl Harbor, attack on, 13
Pennsylvania, hijacked plane crashing in, 5, 8, 119
Pentagon, terrorist attack on the, 3, 5, 6–8, 10, *11*, 12, 15
Philippines, 99, 116
Polo, Marco, 73
Popular Front for the Liberation of Palestine, 28
Powell, Colin, *122*

Qatar, 66
Qur'an, 39, 42, 44–45, 49, 50, 63, 87, 99, 100, *102*, 104

religion and terrorism, 31–32
    Islam, *see* Islam (Muslims), extremist
remembering 9/11, 124
resentment of the United States in the Middle East, 60–69,
        99, 123–24
    for dominating its markets, 62
    Iran and explosion of, 67–68, 69
    for meddling in their politics, 64–66
    prosperity of America and, 61
    by radical Muslims believing Islam is at war with non-
        believers, 71
    for supporting Israel, 61, 65, 70

for supporting oppressive governments, 59, 61, 66
value systems and, 63
Sadat, Anwar, 113
Saudi Arabia, 53, 56, 58, 62, 114
aid to mujaheddin of Afghanistan, 77
bin Laden exiled from, 95, 112
Gulf War and, 56, 68, 112
Saudi Bin Laden Group, 109–10
shahada, 38
sharia (Islamic law), 45, 100, 104
Shi'ites, 47, 91, 106
Somalia, 112, 114
Soviet Union:
Afghanistan and, 32, 76–82, 110, 122
Cold War, see Cold War
Sudan, 95, 112, 114
Sufism, 47
sunna, 45
Sunni Muslims, 47
Suqami, Satam, 17
suras, 44, 63, 104

Tajiks, 74, 91
Taliban, 43, 72, 84–97
beginnings of, 85
bin Laden and, 95, 114
composition of, 84, 86
fall of, 95–97, 116, 123
life under the, 91–94
radical interpretation of Islam, 86–88
rise to power, 83, 85–86
takeover of Afghanistan, 88–90
underground schools for girls, 93
women, treatment of, 88, 92–94
Temple Mount, 52, 53
terrorism, 24–35, 124
fear as goal of, 16, 24–25
history of, 26–27
religion and, 31–32
targets of, 26–27
in the U.S., 13–14

ulema, 105
understanding beliefs and values of other cultures, 123–24
United Nations, 68, 123

United States:
abandonment of Afghans after Soviet withdrawal, 82–83, 122–23
aid to mujaheddin of Afghanistan, 77–78, 79–80
changes since September 11th, 117–24
Cold War, see Cold War
helping each other after 9/11, 118–19
marketing of products in the Middle East, 62
military forces and bases in the Middle East, 56, 60–61, 66, 68–70, 112
patriotism in, 117–18
as peace negotiator in the Middle East, 65, 121–22
resentment in Middle East of, see resentment of the United States in the Middle East
role in the world, 121–23
Taliban defeat and, 96, 116, 123
values, exporting of, 62–63
Urban II, Pope, 49
Uzbeks, 91

value systems, clash of American and Islamic, 62, 63, 124

Wahhabbism, 47–48
War of 1812, 13
women:
Islamic beliefs toward, 42–43, 100
Taliban treatment of, 88, 92–94
World Trade Center, xiv, 7
terrorist attacks on, 1–2, 5, 6, 9–10
changes in America since attack, 117–24
collapse of twin towers, 3, 9–10
facts about the twin towers, 8
history of World Trade Center, 9
identification of bodies, 13
search for survivors, 12
symbolism of, 15–16
terrorist attack in 1993, 9

Yamasaki, Minoru, 9, 16
Yemen, 99, 114, 115, 116

Zubaydah, Abu, 113